SINGER

SEWING REFERENCE LIBRARY™

Timesaving Sewing

Cy DeCosse Incorporated
Minnetonka, Minnesota

SINGER
SEWING REFERENCE LIBRARY™

Timesaving Sewing

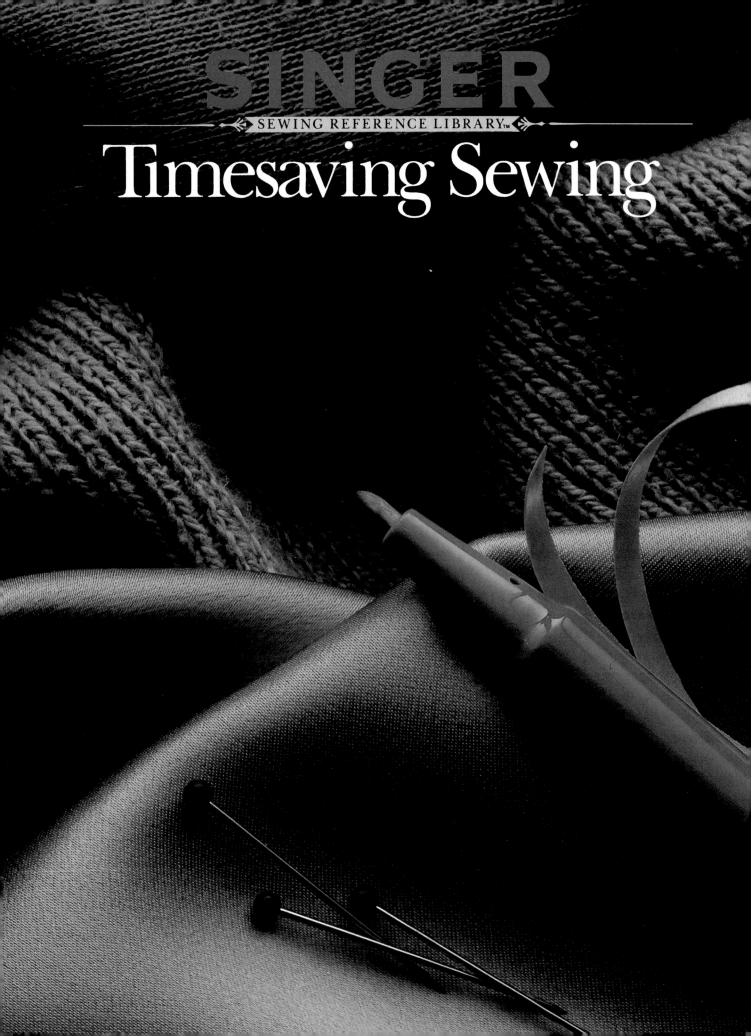

Contents

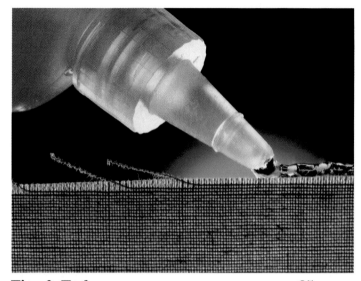

Copyright © 1987
Cy DeCosse Incorporated
5900 Green Oak Drive
Minnetonka, Minnesota 55343
All rights reserved
Printed in U.S.A.

Also available from the publisher: *Sewing
Essentials, Sewing for the Home, Clothing Care
& Repair, Sewing for Style, Sewing Specialty
Fabrics, Sewing Activewear, The Perfect Fit*

Library of Congress
Cataloging-in-Publication Data

Timesaving Sewing

(Singer Sewing Reference Library)
Includes index.
1. Machine sewing. I. Cy DeCosse
Incorporated. II. Series
TT713.T56 1987 646.2'044 87-649
ISBN 0-86573-215-9
ISBN 0-86573-216-7 (pbk.)

Distributed by: Contemporary Books, Inc.
   Chicago, Illinois

CY DE COSSE INCORPORATED
Chairman: Cy DeCosse
President: James B. Maus
Executive Vice President: William B. Jones

TIMESAVING SEWING
Created by: The Editors of Cy DeCosse
   Incorporated, in cooperation with the
   Singer Education Department. Singer is a
   trademark of The Singer Company and is
   used under license.

Managing Editor: Reneé Dignan
Project Director: Gail Devens

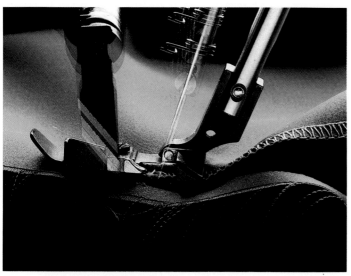

Shortcut Techniques 53

Home Decorating 99

Art Director: Lisa Rosenthal
Writer: Peggy Bendel
Editors: Susan Meyers, Bernice Maehren
Sample Supervisor: Carol Neumann
Technical Photo Director: Bridget Haugh
Sewing Staff: Phyllis Galbraith, Bridget
  Haugh, Kathy Ellingson, Wendy Fedie,
  Rita Opseth
Photographers: Tony Kubat, John Lauenstein,
  Mette Nielsen, Rex Irmen, Bill Lindner,
  Graham Brown
Production Manager: Jim Bindas
Assistant Production Manager: Julie Churchill

Production Staff: Janice Cauley, Joe Fahey,
  Michele Joy, Yelena Konrardy, Carol
  McMall, Dave Schelitzche, Linda
  Schloegel, Cathleen Shannon, Jennie
  Smith, Greg Wallace, Nik Wogstad
Consultants: Zoe Graul, Ann Hurt, Judy
  Lindahl, Barbara Weiland O'Connell, Rita
  Opseth, Belle Rivers, Cheryl Wanska
Contributing Manufacturers: B. Blumenthal;
  Closet Maid by Clairson International;
  Clothilde; Coats & Clark; Dritz
  Corporation; Dyno Merchandise
  Corporation; Everitt Knitting Company;

EZ International; Gosling Tapes; JHB
International; June Tailor, Incorporated;
Lace Country; Minnetonka Mills, Inc.;
Pellon Corporation; Seams Great Products,
Inc.; Sew Easy Textiles, Inc.; The Singer
Company; Stacy Industries, Inc.; Swiss
Metrosene, Inc.; YLI Corporation
Color Separations: Spectrum, Inc.
Printing: W. A. Kreuger (0687)
Home decorating fabrics from Waverly
  Division of F. Schumacher & Co.

How to Use This Book

Timesaving Sewing shows you how to sew more in less time. It is a collection of tips, tools, and techniques adapted from industrial manufacturers, professional dressmakers, and fashion designers who sew with an eye on the clock. This quick and easy style of sewing is an alternative to the more traditional, time-consuming approach. If you enjoy sewing but have trouble fitting it into a busy schedule, you will surely benefit from the shortcuts featured in this book.

Update Your Skills & Equipment

To sew efficiently, you may need to learn new habits and break some old ones. *Timesaving Sewing* begins with a guide to planning, so you get the most value from your sewing time. For example, instead of buying on impulse, be selective so the items you create build a versatile wardrobe. To make every minute count, shop with a plan, select easy-to-sew fabrics, discipline yourself to stockpile only the most useful supplies, and set up a permanent place to sew.

As you think about how to make your sewing area work best for you, explore the recent advances in sewing equipment. New electronic sewing machines offer push-button convenience and built-in stitches that can save you large amounts of time. As a second piece of sewing equipment, the overlock machine, or serger, cuts sewing time even further because it trims raw edges and sews at the same time. It sews at twice the speed of a conventional machine and will help you sew more productively.

Whether or not you decide to invest in a new sewing machine, there are many inexpensive tools and notions that can help you save time. Using a rotary cutter can be a first step toward discovering how fast and easy sewing can be. See how other notions, aids, and supplies can help you achieve professional results in the least amount of time.

Learn Shortcut Dressmaking Methods

From making easy pattern modifications to sewing without pins, there are numerous ways you can save time when constructing garments. Instead of using the general directions on the pattern guidesheet, you can form your own more specific construction plan. You can sew a garment totally with timesaving methods, or you can combine timesaving and traditional methods within a garment, depending on the fabric you have chosen and the style of the garment. *Timesaving Sewing* presents choices so you can decide how to handle specific garment areas, such as sleeves, collars, and hems. The book gives comparable techniques for conventional and overlock sewing machines wherever possible.

Tap the full potential of your sewing machine by learning how to use special presser feet, stitch settings, and attachments. Learn how to adjust the tensions on an overlock machine. On any machine, it takes time to learn the capabilities and practice the techniques, but the time spent pays off in the long run. You will finish faster whenever you can substitute a machine method for handwork.

For greater clarity, contrasting thread is sometimes used to make the stitches more visible in the photos; for most of your own sewing, however, you will need to use matching thread.

Decorate Your Home Quickly & Easily

The final section of *Timesaving Sewing* provides a source of decorating ideas and shows you how to use your dressmaking skills to beautify your home. Learn about products such as self-styling heading tapes and fabrics that are easy to sew.

There are quick methods for curtains, valances, swags, placemats, napkins, and pillow coverings. Most require less than precise measuring, marking, or stitching, but all have a custom look.

Above all, *Timesaving Sewing* shows how fast and easy sewing methods can produce attractive, professional results. Whether you sew items to wear or beautiful soft furnishings for your home, you can accomplish your sewing with minimal time and effort.

rounded,
Padded shoulder

headband

ivory
jewelry

monochromatic
color
coordination

flowing
linen

2½ yards
45" wide
(For skirt, jacket & pants)

1½ yards
- 45" wide

Sewing with a Plan

Plan Your Sewing Time

No matter how busy you are, if you enjoy sewing you can find the time for it. The key is managing your time and possibly changing some sewing habits. For example, if you wait to sew until you have an entire day or evening free, it may be difficult to find the time on a regular basis, but it is much easier if you plan shorter 15 or 20-minute sewing periods.

This kind of time limit might allow you to complete only one sewing step, but that is one step closer to completing a project. If you sew just one seam or detail a day, you can finish a simple skirt in less than a week or a blouse in less than two. You also will find that sewing frequently instead of sporadically keeps you in practice. You can work faster when your sewing skills are in top form than when they are rusty.

Another way to find time is to make sewing a priority. Mark sewing on your calendar as an appointment. Juggle other activities and obligations around the time you have set aside to sew. Choose a time when you are at your peak. This might be the first thing in the morning when you feel most energetic or in the evening when you can relax without interruptions.

During your best time of day you will make fewer mistakes and sew more efficiently.

Manage Sewing in Stages

Whether you spend small or large blocks of time sewing, it is easier to manage the time wisely when you break a sewing project into three general stages: creative, preparation, and construction. During the creative stage, browse for ideas, shop for fabric and patterns, and purchase all supplies. Preparation includes preshrinking the fabric, making fitting adjustments on the pattern, laying out the pattern, cutting, and marking. The construction stage involves sewing, pressing, and fitting.

These three stages take place in different locations. The creative part is essentially a shopping trip outside your home. Preparation for sewing can be done anywhere in your home that is convenient. Construction must be done where your sewing and pressing equipment is set up. To eliminate unnecessary steps between these locations, complete each stage before proceeding to the next. If you are planning

How to Find Time to Sew

Schedule sewing time like any other appointment. As little as 15 minutes is all you need to make progress. It is better to sew briefly and frequently than to sew once in a while for hours. Regular practice keeps skills in top form so you can sew faster with fewer mistakes.

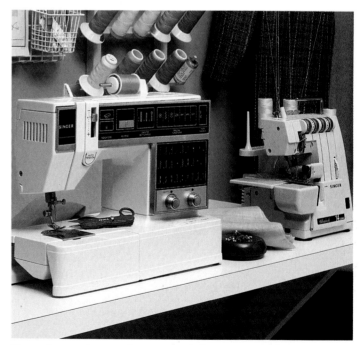

Organize sewing equipment so it is permanently set up and ready to use. Getting sewing tools out and putting them away each time you sew wastes valuable time and energy. Even if space is limited, you can create an inviting sewing area that helps you make wise use of your time.

several projects, dovetail them. Bring all projects through the creative and preparatory phases as a group. You will make good use of shopping time and have one mess instead of several to clean up after layout and cutting.

Keep track of the three sewing stages by making a list. Write down what must be done to bring a project to the next stage. Cross out entries on the list as you complete them. Thus, you will have a record of your progress as well as a reminder of what comes next. After using lists for several projects, you will have developed an efficient way of working and can make mental lists in the future.

Tips for Managing Time

Take pattern instruction sheets along on appointments or when traveling. Use waiting time to study layout diagrams and other directions. Note timesaving techniques or notions you plan to use.

Purchase all sewing supplies before you start. If you run out of an essential mid-project, you will waste time and lose momentum with an extra shopping trip.

Preshrink fabric and other supplies immediately after returning from shopping. Label them so you will remember they are ready to cut.

Sew the newest pattern and fabric first. They are the most inspiring and will give you a positive attitude.

Set realistic deadlines. If you have a short time, plan to complete no more than one or two sewing steps.

Dovetail projects. Shop for several projects in one trip. Lay out, cut, and mark as a group. Group items that require the same thread color so you can sew without stopping to wind new bobbins.

Delegate difficult sewing to a dressmaker.

Try team sewing or working with others in an assembly line when you must make a quantity of items, such as for holiday gifts or bazaars.

Plan sewing projects by dividing work into three stages. First stage includes all creative decisions and purchases. Second stage involves preparations such as preshrinking, making pattern adjustments, cutting, laying out, and marking. Final stage is construction sewing and pressing. Finish one stage completely before proceeding to the next.

List things to do for planned sewing projects. Then check off each item when it is completed. You will have an encouraging record of your progress and will not waste time by forgetting anything.

Plan a Sewing Area

To sew conveniently and efficiently, find space for a permanent sewing area. It is not essential to devote an entire room to sewing. Comfortable and practical setups can fit into a corner, an alcove, a closet, or a multipurpose room. In fact, it is easier to organize a small space than a large one. A compact area also allows you to arrange everything within arm's reach.

It is ideal to concentrate cutting, sewing, and pressing equipment in one, U-shaped place. If there is not enough space for everything, locate the cutting area elsewhere. Give priority to arranging sewing and pressing equipment side by side. Lower the ironing board or pressing table to a height you can use while seated. Then you can alternate between sewing and pressing without taking a step.

Modular storage systems such as those designed for closets or offices are adaptable to sewing areas and can be arranged to fit the available space. Open or transparent storage units allow you to see everything at a glance and make supplies easily accessible. When the sewing area is not in use, conceal it behind closed doors, roller shades, or a folding screen. Avoid room arrangements that require moving sewing equipment when you are finished.

How to Organize a Sewing Area

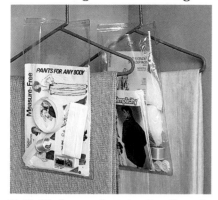

Fold fabric over hanger. Put thread, pattern, notions, and supplies for project in plastic bag. Punch hole in top to hang bag with fabric. After layout and cutting, store garment sections in bag.

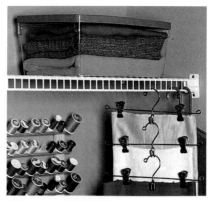

Clip stockpiled fabrics to multiple skirt or pants hangers, and store maximum amount in minimal space. Fold knits and loose weaves; stack on shelves or in drawers to prevent stretching out of shape.

Buy duplicates of basic tools such as marking pen, scissors, magnetic pin cushion, and tape measure. Put each set in plastic caddy. Store one set near cutting area, and the other near sewing/pressing center.

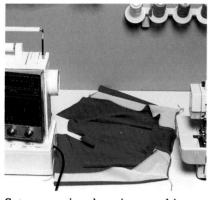

Set conventional sewing machine and overlock machine next to each other. Allow ample work space in between for garment sections.

Adjust office chair on casters to your height for good back support. Swivel between the sewing and pressing areas as you work. Lower ironing board so you can press while seated.

Store used patterns in plastic envelopes; then organize envelopes in portable file box. Divide file into fashion categories for quick storage and retrieval. Discard patterns occasionally to keep system efficient.

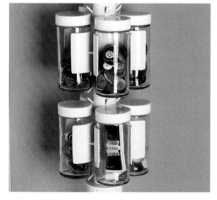

Group notions such as buttons, tapes, and zippers; store them in transparent boxes or jars or in tool chest with clear plastic drawers. Clear containers allow you to locate needed items at a glance.

Roll fusible interfacings on tubes to prevent wrinkling. Store plastic interleaving inside tube to save manufacturer's instructions and to identify interfacing.

Install wall-hung storage units to make the most of available space. Hang tools from hooks. Organize threads on wooden storage racks. Racks are available for overlock cones and all-purpose spools.

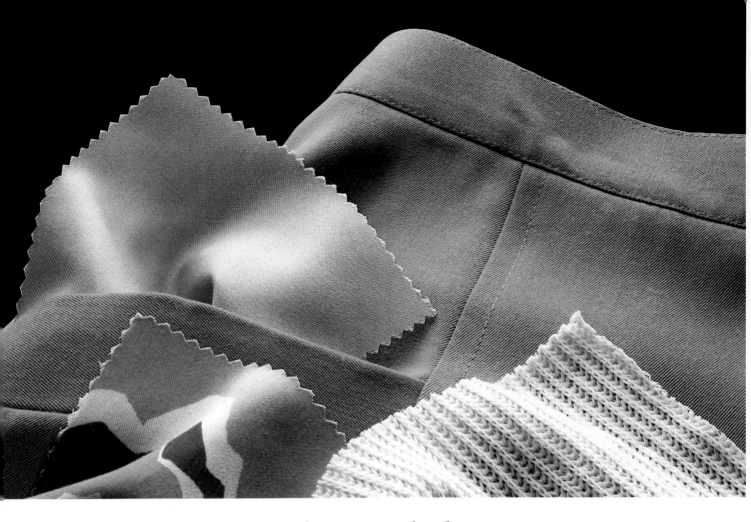

Plan a Season-spanning Wardrobe

If your time is limited, you probably cannot make every item you want or need. Decide what to sew by planning carefully. Garments that offer the best value for your sewing time will be those that suit your lifestyle, skill level, and budget. They should also blend with your current wardrobe, look fashionable, and, for maximum wear, be made from seasonless fabrics and colors.

Analyze Your Wardrobe

Look through your clothes and evaluate them for up-to-date style, comfortable fit, and extent of wear. If some items seem dated, new accessories might freshen their look. If fit is a problem, consider minor alterations such as adding shoulder pads, tapering pants legs, or changing hemlines. Discard items you have not worn in a long time, those needing major alterations, and any beyond repair.

Consider also whether your wardrobe meets your needs for career, home, leisure, and special-occasion activities. Identify gaps in your wardrobe, especially as your lifestyle changes. Plan to spend the bulk of your sewing time on clothes you can wear most often. Many styles can do double duty, such as a

simple dress or a tailored jacket that can be dressed up or down. Make a list of the items necessary to complete and balance your wardrobe.

Study Current Fashion Trends

Browse through retail stores and fashion magazines before each fall/winter and spring/summer sewing season begins. Use what you see to help you style wardrobe additions. Make notes, and gather clippings to record ideas.

Time is wasted if you spend it sewing something that is soon out of date. Look for fashion changes in proportion, fit, and silhouette. Become aware of the new size and shape of details such as pockets, collars, and lapels. Determine the coming key accessories and accent pieces. Take note of prominent colors, color combinations, and fabrics. Imitate and adapt the trend-setting fashions. This will make you feel and look up to date.

Choose Seasonless Fabrics & Colors

Many fabrics can be worn practically year round. Fill out your wardrobe by sewing versatile fashions in

fabrics that span the seasons. These fabrics include knits, denim, wool crepe and gabardine, silk or wool tweed, silk broadcloth, synthetic suede, oxford and chambray shirtings, crepe de chine, tissue faille, challis, and linen weaves. For greatest wearability, avoid very heavy or very lightweight fabrics, which are identified strongly with a single short season. Medium to lightweight fabrics are more appropriate for multi-season wear.

In addition to fabric type and weight, consider color. Choose lightweight spring/summer fabrics in medium to dark tones and heavier fall/winter fabrics in medium to light tones so clothes can make the transition from one season to the next. For example, brown linen is comfortable for the warm weather months but with a change of accessories looks fine when worn in fall because of the midrange color. Turquoise wool gabardine is wearable in early spring and into summer in temperate climates, but is warm enough for winter weather.

Collect Classic Fabrics

Anyone who sews seriously has a stockpile of fabrics, because it is natural to purchase more than can be

sewn in any one season. If your stockpile specializes in fabrics that do not go out of style, it can help you save time. When you want to add to your wardrobe, select the fabrics you need from your personal collection and eliminate a shopping trip.

In general, plain fabrics are less likely to go out of style than highly decorative fabrics. Neutral colors are more long-lasting than unusual fashion colors, unless those fashion colors are your favorites and are mainstays of your wardrobe year after year. Prints usually cannot stand the test of time and may look dated after a single season or two; however, some prints, such as dots and foulards, qualify as classics. Woven or printed stripes and plaids also age gracefully in your fabric collection.

Organize the fabric stockpile to make it accessible. Preshrink fabrics immediately after purchase, and label each piece accordingly. On the label, also note fiber content, width, and length. Cut a sample and keep it in a purse-sized notebook to prevent duplicate purchases and to help coordinate future selections. Store fabrics on hangers or shelves by season, color, or fabric type. Protect your investment in woolens by using an appropriate moth repellent.

Plan What to Buy & What to Sew

If time is short, sew selected garments for your wardrobe and purchase the rest. One way to decide what to sew and what to buy is by degree of difficulty. You will save time by buying wardrobe items that require complicated or involved sewing techniques or that are made in difficult-to-handle fabrics. Concentrate on sewing garments that can be simply constructed.

In general, cardigan jackets, unlined jackets, simple coats and blouses, pants, and skirts may be well worth your sewing time because they can be finished quickly. Lined garments, coats and jackets with tailored details, and closely fitted dresses require a proportionately greater amount of sewing time per item. You could make several simple garments in the time allotted to make one that is more complex.

You may find the items that require more time to sew may also be more expensive. If budget enters into your decisions, determine your priorities by balancing available funds against available time.

Also consider personal preferences when making buy-or-sew decisions. If you enjoy sewing jackets but not blouses, follow your instincts. You will finish the jacket quickly if you enjoy the process, even though more sewing is involved. If you have fitting problems, it may be wiser to sew than to shop at several stores or commit yourself to extensive garment alterations.

The patterns and fabrics you have on hand should also influence your choices. Check patterns you have used before to see if they are suitable for your current needs. Repeating a pattern saves time, because you are familiar with the construction techniques and fitting adjustments have already been made. If your stockpile includes the right fabric for the pattern, you are ready to start sewing.

Shopping Efficiently

Before you shop, focus on what you want to accomplish. With your wardrobe plan in mind, prepare a written list of the items to buy and the items to sew. Keep a swatch notebook including swatches of stockpiled fabrics to coordinate with new purchases. Also include fabric samples from existing wardrobe items. You can usually snip a scrap from the facings or the seam allowances.

Purchase ready-to-wear items first, and then select the supplies for sewing coordinates. You have more flexibility in color, style, and fabric when you sew than when you buy. It is easier to assemble outfits around a purchased item than to sew first and search later for an appropriate ready-made item.

If you do not have time to find everything you need with one shopping trip, confine purchases to items that complete an outfit or group of related separates. Isolated items that remain idle until you find the missing pieces can waste your time and your money. If repeated shopping trips leave you empty-handed, turn to alternative fabric sources to meet your needs.

Fabric Shopping Alternatives

In addition to shopping at local fabric stores, you can purchase fabrics by mail order or through in-home sales representatives. The addresses for these services are in advertisements in fashion sewing magazines.

Mail-order and in-home shopping services are convenient, timesaving ways to purchase sewing supplies. They expose you to a wide range of fabrics. Many also offer patterns, linings, interfacings, zippers, thread, and other sewing accessories. Alternative fabric sources can be an efficient way to fulfill a wardrobe plan, but there are drawbacks. It can be difficult to select fabric from a swatch. It is especially difficult to determine fabric hand and drapability, as well as to judge the true nature of large prints from a small sample. Although most alternative services price fabrics competitively, you must pay shipping charges. You must also wait several days or more until fabrics arrive.

Tips for Fabric Shopping by Mail

Shop with a wardrobe plan and specific patterns in mind. Order what you need, rather than on impulse.

Phone in your order if possible. Many firms have toll-free numbers answered by trained personnel who will be sure to gather all necessary information for quick shipping. Some can even inform you on availability of stock.

Order as soon as possible after receiving a swatch brochure. Supplies are limited, and popular fabrics sell out fast. The sooner you order, the more likely you are to receive your selection.

Take advantage of services that send color-matched linings, thread, and other notions. Save time by ordering everything you need at once.

Check the firm's return policy. Most will accept returns if you are not satisfied, but some charge for returns or consider all sales final.

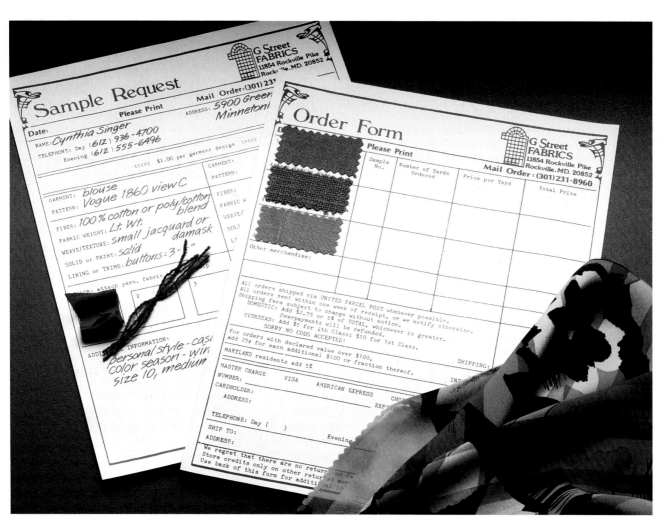

Mail-order service is offered through leading fabric retail stores. Seasonal fabric swatches from current stock are offered for a one-time fee. Some large stores and fabric outlets also sell swatch cards of seasonless fabric classics, such as synthetic suede, wool crepe, and linen, which are available all year. In addition, some stores offer a sample service; you can make specific requests, and they will send swatches tailored to your needs.

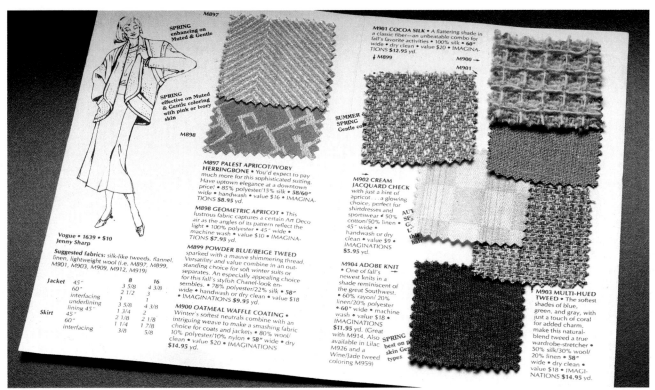

Within the image:

SPRING enhancing on Muted & Gentle

SPRING effective on Muted & Gentle coloring with pink or ivory skin

M897

M898

M897 PALEST APRICOT/IVORY HERRINGBONE • You'd expect to pay much more for this sophisticated suiting. Have uptown elegance at a downtown price! • 85% polyester/15% silk • 58/60" wide • handwash • value $16 • IMAGINA-TIONS $8.95 yd.

M898 GEOMETRIC APRICOT • This lustrous fabric captures a certain Art Deco air as the angles of its pattern reflect the light • 100% polyester • 45″ wide • machine wash • value $10 • IMAGINA-TIONS $7.95 yd.

M899 POWDER BLUE/BEIGE TWEED • sparked with a mauve shimmering thread. Versatility and value combine in an out-standing choice for soft winter suits or separates. An especially appealing choice for this fall's stylish Chanel-look en-sembles. • 78% polyester/22% silk • 58″ wide • handwash or dry clean • value $18 • IMAGINATIONS $9.95 yd.

M900 OATMEAL WAFFLE COATING • Winter's softest neutrals combine with an intriguing weave to make a smashing fabric choice for coats and jackets • 80% wool/10% polyester/10% nylon • 58″ wide • dry clean • value $20 • IMAGINATIONS $14.95 yd.

Vogue • 1639 • $10
Jenny Sharp

Suggested fabrics: silk-like tweeds, flannel, linen, lightweight wool (i.e. M897, M899, M901, M903, M909, M912, M919)

		8	16
Jacket	45″		
	60″	3 5/8	4 3/8
	interfacing	2 1/2	3
	underlining	1	1
	lining 45″	3 5/8	4 3/8
Skirt	45″	1 3/4	2
	60″	2 1/8	2 1/8
	interfacing	1 1/4	1 7/8
		3/8	5/8

M899

M900

M901

M901 COCOA SILK • A flattering shade in a classic fiber—an unbeatable combo for fall's favorite activities • 100% silk • 60″ wide • dry clean • value $20 • IMAGINA-TIONS $12.95 yd.

SUMMER & SPRING Gentle co...

M902 CREAM JACQUARD CHECK • with just a hint of apricot . . . a glowing choice, perfect for shirtdresses and sportswear • 50% cotton/50% linen • 45″ wide • handwash or dry clean • value $9 • IMAGINATIONS $5.95 yd.

M904 ADOBE KNIT • One of fall's newest knits in a shade reminiscent of the great Southwest. • 60% rayon/ 20% linen/20% polyester • 60″ wide • machine wash • value $18 • IMAGINATIONS $11.95 yd. (Great with M914. Also available in Lilac M926 and a Wine/Jade tweed coloring M959)

M903 MULTI-HUED TWEED • The softest shades of blue, green, and gray, with just a touch of coral for added charm, make this natural-blend tweed a true wardrobe-stretcher • 50% silk/30% wool/20% linen • 58″ wide • dry clean • value $18 • IMAGI-NATIONS $14.95 yd.

Fabric clubs offer subscriptions to a swatch service. Four or more times a year you receive brochures with swatches of fabrics currently for sale. Usually these presentations feature coordinated fabric groups and pattern suggestions to help in planning your fabric purchases.

Within the image:

Pag. 75

Tissus **Rénel**

[ ] TOS [ ] LOW [ ] HR [ ] SALE   13-4229
TAN/DEEP BRTS POLY CRNKL DOBBY PRT AU
Price: $ 11.95
Width: 44″

no bleach, optional.

...commend pre-shrinking every fabric to be used on finished garment.

...S IN DEEP BRIGHTS
...crepe de chine takes ...
...dd lustre.

In-home fabric sales are a variation of mail order. A sales representative shows fabric samples in her home and helps you place an order. Samples are mounted on swatch cards, which include information such as fiber content, size of print repeat, and width. Most sales representatives are experienced dressmakers who can give advice and assistance.

Choose Timesaving Patterns

All pattern brands include styles designed for fast sewing. These patterns are indicated with a label or distinctive title on the envelope and catalog page. In some catalogs, timesaving styles are grouped behind a special tab divider so you can find them quickly.

Timesaving patterns can be skill-related, time-related, or both. Skill-related patterns are identified for beginners, or they have a term such as "easy" in the title. The instruction sheet uses only basic sewing techniques. Of course, you do not have to be a novice to use such patterns. If you have some sewing experience, you can be sure the pattern will not take you much time to sew.

Time-related patterns have terms such as "fast," "3-hour," or "jiffy" in their labels. Each pattern company has its own standards of what qualifies a pattern for this category, but generally these patterns have a minimum number of pieces. They also have a minimum number of details, and complicated or difficult constructions have been omitted. Easy-to-handle fabrics are suggested, and shortcuts such as fusible interfacing and flat construction methods may be given in the sewing instructions.

Overlock patterns are also timesavers. These patterns are especially suitable for sewing on an overlock machine. Overlock patterns from major companies can also be sewn on a conventional sewing machine, so dual construction methods are included. Specialty pattern companies design for overlock sewing to a greater degree and offer patterns that can be sewn entirely on an overlock machine.

If there is not a timesaving pattern in the style you are searching for, be sure to look at other patterns in the catalog. Many regular patterns miss meeting a company's timesaving criteria because of a minor point such as collar styling or one too many pattern pieces. The pattern may still be relatively timesaving. Also, to save time, you can modify the details or construction methods as you like. Give yourself the broadest possible fashion choice by considering the full range of pattern offerings and evaluating the time factor before you purchase, if time is a consideration.

Guide to Selecting Timesaving Patterns

	Timesaving	Average	Time-consuming
Fit	Very loose, loose	Semi-fitted	Fitted, closely fitted
Neckline	Ribbing trim	Faced	Shaped band, bound
Collar	Convertible	Shawl, standing, flat	Notched, rolled shirt
Sleeve	Cut-on cap, kimono, dolman	Raglan, shirt, dropped shoulder	Set-in
Sleeve finish	Hemmed, buttoned	Band cuff	Shirt cuff, bound placket
Waistline	Elasticized casing	Waistband with closure concealed in pocket	Waistband with zipper, buttoned closure
Pockets	In-seam, patch	Side slant	Welt, flapped
Hem	Straight or A-line; fused or machine-stitched	Slightly flared; twin-needle topstitched	Full, gathered, or pleated; hand sewn
Closure	Pullover	Zipper, hook and loop tape	Buttons with buttonholes
Details	Topstitching, edgestitching, twin-needle topstitching	Darts, gathers, linings, bands, unpressed pleats	Shaped inserts, pressed pleats, tabs, flaps, tailored vents, piping or other seam insertions

Tips for Selecting Timesaving Patterns

Look at the number of pattern pieces. The more pieces there are, the more time it takes for layout, cutting, and sewing.

Judge the degree of fit. The more closely fitted the style, the more time required for pattern adjustments and fine-tuning alterations — especially if your figure varies from the standard pattern sizing.

Analyze the details. Patch pockets are easier to sew than welt pockets. Pressed pleats require more steps than unpressed pleats. Pullover or wrap styles that require no closures will save you time.

Analyze the construction. Shaped inserts and eased areas take more time than simple seams. Straps or belts that must be stitched and turned right side out could take an entire sewing session. Plan to spend extra time whenever a seam or edge requires reinforcement stitching or clipping.

Decide if you can simplify the pattern to save time. If you can add shortcuts without sacrificing style or quality, your pattern choice is less limited.

Think about whether the pattern lends itself to future use. Many patterns have multiple views with a choice of details, such as necklines and sleeves, so you can repeat the pattern for a variety of looks. Using a familiar pattern pays off by saving you fitting and sewing time.

Choose Timesaving Fabrics

Several fabrics are probably appropriate for any pattern you choose. Select fabrics that are easy to work with and you will save time. Avoid fabrics that require extensive preparation, complicated layout, special handling, or extra finishing and construction steps. This does not mean you must confine yourself to dull, boring choices. It takes no more time to sew a beautiful fabric than an ordinary one, and many fabrics with texture or attractive printed designs satisfy timesaving requirements. In fact, the more interesting the fabric you choose, the simpler the pattern style can and should be.

As you shop for fabrics, keep in mind their suitability for shortcut construction techniques. For example, fusible interfacings cannot be used on fabrics sensitive to heat or stained by moisture. A bulky or heavy fabric does not lend itself to cut-on pockets or facings. On the other hand, in an effort to avoid edge finishing, do not automatically reject fabrics that ravel; a timesaving technique using precut tricot bias binding can make an easy and attractive edge finish.

Guide to Selecting Timesaving Fabrics

	Fabric	Special Texture	Type of Interfacing	Edge Finish Required	Ease of Pressing	Other Considerations
Timesaving	**Broadcloth**		Fusible or sew-in	Usually	Easy	
	Double, interlock knits	One-way shading	Fusible or sew-in	Rarely	Average	
	Lace	Sheer, may have one-way design	None required	Rarely	Easy	Borders may be used as prefinished edge.
	Oxford or chambray shirting		Fusible or sew-in	Usually	Easy	
	Poplin		Fusible or sew-in	Usually	Easy	
	Silk noile	One-way shading	Fusible or sew-in	Usually	Easy	
	Sweater knits	Bulky	None required	Rarely	Easy	
Moderate	**Challis**	Slippery	Fusible or sew-in	Always	Easy	
	Eyelet	Open embroidery, may have one-way design	Sew-in or none	Usually	Easy	Borders may be used as prefinished edge.
	Flannel	Napped	Fusible or sew-in	Usually	Average	
	Gabardine	One-way shading	Fusible or sew-in	Usually	Difficult	
	Linen		Fusible or sew-in	Always	Easy	
	Piqué		Sew-in	Usually	Average	
	Tricot	Slippery	None required	None required	Easy	Raw edges tend to curl.
	Tweed		Fusible or sew-in	Usually	Easy	Line for comfort and stability.
	Velveteen	Napped	Fusible or sew-in	Usually	Average	
Time Consuming	**Acetate taffeta, satin**	Slippery	Sew-in	Always	Difficult	Water-spot; do not ease well.
	Brocade, metallics, sequined fabrics	One-way shading	Sew-in	Always	Difficult	Line or underline; test metallics before pressing; do not press sequined fabric.
	Charmeuse	Slippery, one-way shading	Sew-in or self-lining	Always	Difficult	Extreme care is needed in every sewing step.
	Corduroy	Napped, some are bulky	Fusible or sew-in	Always	Average	Lighter weight corduroys are easier to handle.
	Crepe de chine	Slippery	Fusible or sew-in	Always	Average	
	Denim	One-way color shading, some are bulky	Fusible or sew-in	Always	Average	
	Fake fur	Bulky, napped	None required	Rarely	None required	Cut out single layer; must free nap from seams by hand.
	Shantung	One-way color shading, slippery	Fusible or sew-in	Always	Average	
	Synthetic suede	Napped	Fusible or sew-in	None required	Average; needs special handling	Requires special construction methods.
	Tissue faille	Slippery	Fusible or sew-in	Always	Average	
	Velvet	Slippery, napped	Sew-in	Always	Difficult	

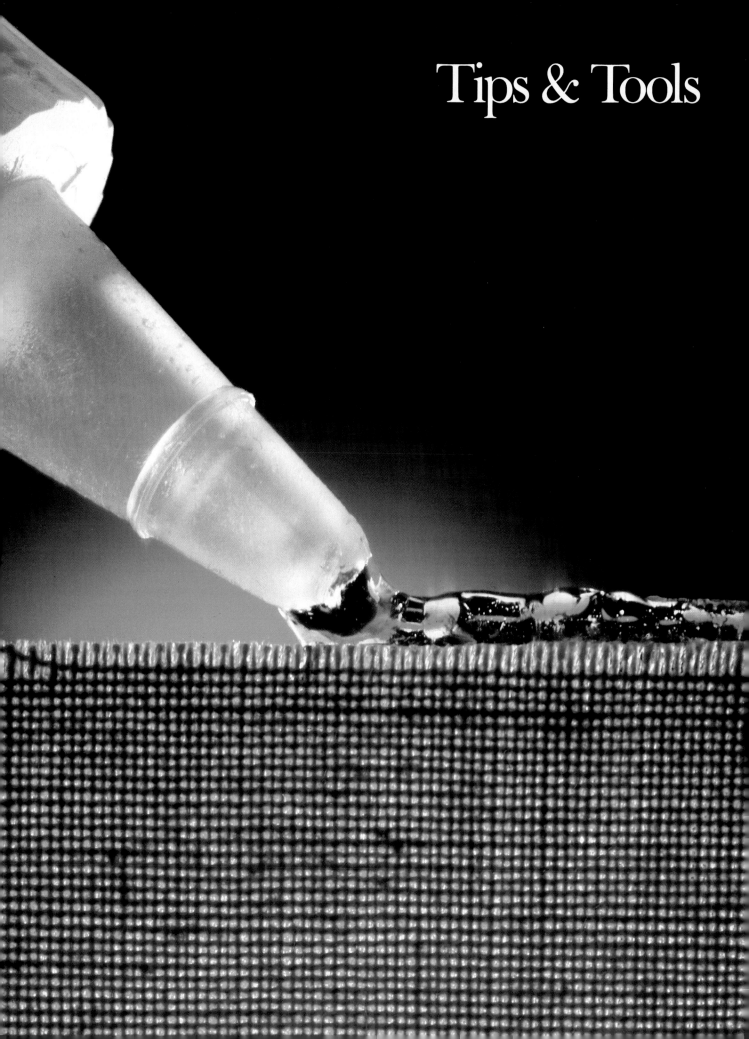

Stockpiling Notions & Equipment

New tools and notions are constantly being developed to streamline sewing. Check store displays periodically to keep abreast of what is available. You will often find worthwhile items to help you sew more efficiently.

Keep on hand a supply of often-used notions and other basic items. You will have a shorter shopping list for every project and will not interrupt your sewing by suddenly running out of an essential item. Watch for sales, so you can assemble supplies at bargain prices.

Stockpile with a plan. In addition to basic black, white, navy, and beige, most people have favorite colors they choose repeatedly for their wardrobes. If there are colors you choose most often, stock up on threads, zippers, tapes, buttons, and linings accordingly. Keep track of what you have, and replenish supplies before you run out. For the serger, keep cone thread in basic colors.

Fusible interfacings are frequently used in timesaving sewing. Rather than purchasing a short length of fusible interfacing for each project, buy longer cuts in a range of weights and types. You cannot predict how fusible interfacing will work with the fabric unless you make a test sample before you cut. Stockpiled interfacings allow you to test-fuse a variety and select the best for the project.

As you collect basic supplies, also stock replacement parts such as overlock knives and machine needles. With a fresh knife or needle always on hand, you can service equipment without interrupting sewing progress.

Notions	Fabrics	Replacement Parts	Timesaving Tools
Buttons in black, white, off-white, and navy are appropriate for many projects. Sew-through buttons can be applied by machine. When using unique buttons, purchase one extra so if one is lost you do not have to replace an entire set.	**Fusible web** with paper backing, or web to be used with transfer sheet, is convenient for hemming, machine appliqué, and many home decorating projects. Purchase web in at least 5 yd. (5 m) cuts to have sufficient amount for large or small applications.	**Blades** for rotary cutter become dull or nicked through use. Keep spare package of replacement blades on hand.	**Basting tape** allows you to position seams, zippers, hems, or trims without pinning or handbasting. Dissolvable basting tape does not require separate step to remove from washable garments.
Elastic is used frequently for casings. Stock most commonly used widths — ¼", ⅜", ½", and 1" (6, 10, 13, and 24 mm).	**Interfacings** should be purchased in at least 5 yd. (5 m) lengths to be used for several garments. Assemble variety of types and colors, including precut fusibles for cuffs, waistbands, and hems.	**Bobbins** can be purchased by the dozen so you always have plenty. Wind bobbins in advance for large projects. Store filled bobbins with matching spools so they are ready for sewing.	**Glue stick** substitutes for basting or pinning to hold zippers, seams, or trims in position for stitching.
Heavy-duty hook and eye closures can be used instead of buttoned closures. Also keep snaps and sets of hooks and eyes on hand.	**Linings** can be purchased from remnant tables in 1½ to 2 yd. (1.5 to 2 m) lengths, which are sufficient for most jackets and skirts. Choose silky polyesters and other blouse or dress weight fabrics, which wear better than acetate linings. Save large scraps for pocket linings. Lining does not have to match garment fabric exactly, so it is practical to stockpile black, white, and beige or other basic wardrobe colors.	**Knives on overlock machine** can become dull or damaged. Consult manual to determine whether upper or lower knife requires more frequent replacement, and keep an extra knife on hand.	**Liquid fray preventer** seals and reinforces fabric cut edges and secures stitching.
Precut fusible web strips are handy for tacking facings, fusing hems, and positioning trims, pockets, or appliqués.		**Sewing machine bulb** lasts a long time, but inevitably burns out at inconvenient moment. Purchase spare bulb to be prepared.	**Magnetic pin cushion** keeps steel pins, scissors, seam ripper, and thimble handy. Also use to pick up pins from floor and to clear sewing area.
Precut tricot bias binding has multiple uses as edge finish and casing. It easily curls over fabric edge, so it can be stitched without pinning or basting. Keep black, white, and beige on hand for nearly invisible finish on many colors.	**Underlinings** in black, white, and beige are suitable for most fashion fabrics. Because the decision to underline may be made during preparation stage rather than creative stage of a sewing project, it is convenient to have a choice of underlinings available.	**Sewing machine needles** in three sizes will meet most sewing needs — size 11 (75) for lightweight fabrics, size 14 (90) for medium weights, and size 16 (100) for heavy weights. Have a reserve of conventional and overlock needles.	**Marking pen** with water-soluble or evaporating ink makes temporary markings that require no extra step for removal.
Shoulder pads provide quick fitting adjustments and fashion shaping. Have a variety of pad shapes and thicknesses on hand.			**Pressurized air** quickly cleans lint and other debris from overlock machine.
Thread, in most often used colors, is essential item to stockpile. Collect same colors in cones and spools; Polyester/cotton or 100% polyester all-purpose thread meets most sewing needs. Avoid overstocking thread; like all textiles, thread deteriorates with age.			**Rotary cutter** is home-size cutting tool adapted from industry; it cuts faster than traditional shears. Protect cutter and work surface with special plastic mat under pattern and fabric.
Zippers in 9" (23 cm) length and in basic colors can be used for most skirts and pants. Shorten, if necessary.			**Seam ripper** prong slips under stitches; sharp edge cuts threads for quick removal.
			Thread snips with spring-action blades can be picked up quickly and will cut in any position.
			Weights hold pattern pieces in place for layout and cutting. They are more efficient than pins, especially for large, less intricate pattern pieces.

Choosing & Using Thread

Although thread may seem like a minor sewing notion, it is an important one. Avoid discount types, and pay a little more for name-brand quality. Good quality thread looks smooth, resists breaking, and is uniform in color, diameter, and twist. Inferior thread can cause stitching problems and result in a garment that comes apart at the seams.

Choose thread according to the fabric weight and fiber content as well as for the machine you are using, conventional or overlock. The finer the weave or knit and the lighter the fabric weight, the smaller in diameter the thread should be. Use extra-fine thread, sometimes called embroidery or lingerie thread, on delicate and sheer fabrics. Use all-purpose thread for most other fabrics.

The fiber content of the thread and the fabric do not have to match, but cotton or silk threads should be used only on woven fabrics made from cotton, linen, silk, or wool fibers. Cotton/polyester and all-polyester threads are general-purpose; use them on natural or synthetic fibers, knits or wovens.

Although general-purpose threads can be used on either a conventional or an overlock machine, it is a good idea to use special overlock threads on an overlock machine. These threads, wound on tubes or cones, provide the large quantities of thread required for overlock stitching. Also, these threads are usually smaller in diameter — between the weight of all-purpose and extra-fine — to help create a smooth, flat seam or hem. Finally, good quality overlock threads are designed to create minimal lint, and some are finished with an industrial-type lubricant for high-speed sewing.

Tips on Thread

Purchase basic and favorite thread colors in large, economy-size spools, tubes, or cones. Purchase small spools of thread in current fashion colors or for special sewing projects.

Purchase enough thread for the project at hand. For a conventional machine, one 120 yd. (114 m) spool of thread is enough for most tops, skirts, and pants. Two spools are necessary for most dresses, jackets, and jumpsuits. Three spools or one large 325 yd. (309 m) spool is required for most separates patterns. Estimate thread for home decorating projects by figuring that 100 yds. (95 m) of thread will stitch 30 ft. (9.5 m) at 10 to 12 stitches per inch (2.5 cm).

Store threads by color for easy selection, and label with purchase date. Make a point of using thread as quickly as possible. Old threads can break, fade, and mildew.

Choose thread color that is one shade darker than fabric. Match background color of plaids, tweeds, and prints. Purchase your thread at the same time you purchase fabric.

Make needle threading easier by painting shaft of presser foot white or affixing white tape to shaft immediately behind needle area. For overlock threading, use tweezers to pull thread through eye of needle.

Avoid excessive stockpile of overlock threads by matching only needle thread to fabric. This is the only thread that could show from right side of garment. On overlock machines with two needles, use matching thread in left-hand needle. Use blending colors to thread the loopers and second needle.

Hand-sew with single strand of thread about 20" (51 cm) long. Shorter strands are used up too quickly, especially when you are sewing hems or several buttons. Longer strands tend to knot and tangle.

Draw thread through slot of plastic container to coat with beeswax for hand sewing. Coated thread does not tangle, and stitches stay firmly in place.

Cut thread diagonally from spool, and thread needle with cut end. Do not moisten cut end of polyester thread; moisture swells plies and makes needle more difficult to thread.

Prevent thread from catching in notch on base of spool and possibly breaking by aiming notch in opposite direction from which thread is drawn.

Wind several bobbins before you start sewing, so you will not have to stop and fill partway through. Make sure bobbin is full before making machine buttonholes.

Timesaving Layout & Cutting Aids

Save time during pattern layout and cutting by using the fewest possible pins or eliminating pins entirely. For cutting, use weights to hold the pattern on the fabric. Purchase sets of sewing weights, or improvise by using canned goods. To lay out a pattern with weights, arrange large pattern pieces first, then small ones. Pin through grainline markings on large pattern pieces. Place weights on one pattern piece at a time, inside the cutting line.

Use a rotary cutter instead of shears to speed the work. This tool works like a pizza cutter. The sharp wheel cuts easily through multiple layers of fabric so patterns can be cut out in a few, swift motions. Protect the cutting edge and work surface by using a special plastic mat under the fabric. Mats are available in several types and sizes. The most practical is as large as your layout surface. Those printed with a grid and bias lines can save time, because you can use the printed lines to help you measure accurately. Also use the rotary cutter to trim pattern margins before cutting and to trim seam allowances from interfacings.

How to Use a Rotary Cutter

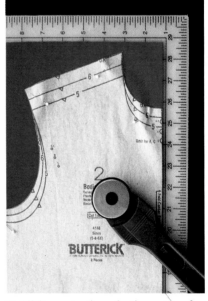

1) Slide protective plastic mat under pattern piece to be cut. Shift mat under pattern pieces as needed, so work surface is always covered as you cut.

2) Use a metal ruler as a guide for cutting straight edges. Hold rotary cutter so thumb is on blade side of handle. Trim off notches as you cut. Blades are adjustable for cutting lightweight fabric or heavy, bulky, and multiple layers.

3) Use small rotary cutter for short, straight lines and sharp curves. Small wheel is easier to maneuver than large one when cutting lines have complex shapes.

Timesaving Basting Aids

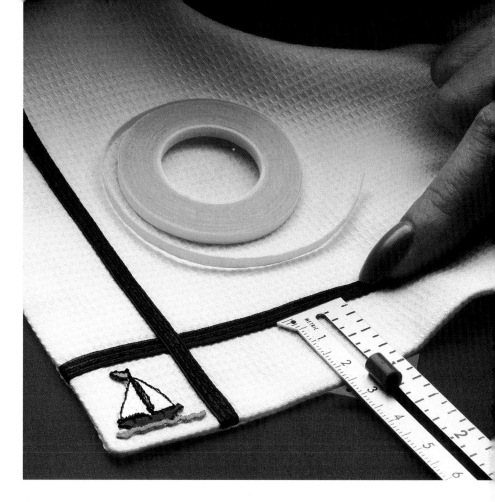

Basting can be a time-consuming preparation for final stitching. Yet it becomes especially important if you are sewing a garment on an overlock machine, because you may want to baste first to check the fit. After seams are overlocked, there is no seam allowance left to provide a margin for error if the seams have to be let out.

Adhesives, fusibles, machine speed basting (page 61), and dissolvable basting thread (page 32) are fast alternatives to hand sewing or pinning. Use these techniques for making seams and hems, inserting zippers, and positioning trims and details.

How to Use Timesaving Basting Aids

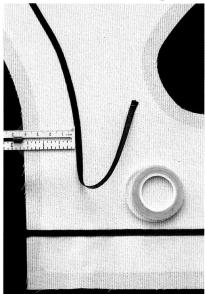

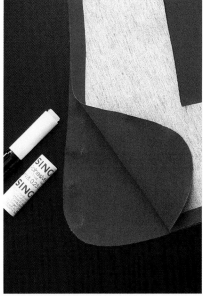

Basting tape. Use to position trims, appliqués, zippers, and pockets. With adhesive side down, finger press in position desired. Remove paper backing from face of tape to expose adhesive. Position detail, and stitch in position; do not stitch through tape. Water-soluble tape will dissolve in first washing.

Glue stick. Apply dots of glue to seam allowances of first fabric layer so glue is next to, but not on, stitching line. While glue is still tacky, position second layer. Use glue sparingly. Refrigerate stick in warm or humid weather to keep it firm.

Fusible web. Fold ¼ yd. (.25 m) of fusible web several times to cut ⅛" (3 mm) strips. To attach patch pockets, slip strip under edge of pocket, and press onto garment before stitching. Pocket will not shift as you stitch. You can also use web to baste appliqués and trims.

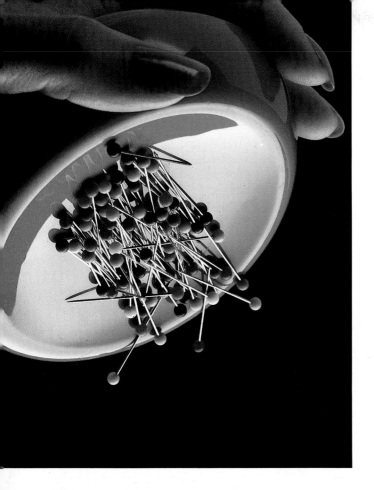

Timesaving Sewing Aids

Timesaving sewing aids solve specific sewing problems or make techniques easier. Many of these aids are versatile and can save time in ways other than the specific purposes for which they were designed. A magnetic pin cushion, for example, not only holds steel pins and needles but is handy for cleanup, too; just slide it along the sewing surface or nearby floor area to attract stray pins and needles. Hook and loop tape, often used for closures, can also be used to attach shoulder pads.

Sewing aids are continually being developed. Many, such as liquid fray preventer and fusible web, rely on adhesive, chemical, or heat-sensitive formulations to replace handwork. When using one of these sewing aids for the first time, test on scraps to develop a feeling for using the aid.

Periodically check fabric stores and notions counters for newer products, such as dissolvable basting thread; and look for new designs of products that are updated often, such as iron-on appliqués. Not all timesaving sewing aids are recent innovations, however. Do not overlook the timesaving capabilities of tried-and-true tools such as the seam ripper, button spacer, and thread snips.

How to Use Timesaving Sewing Aids

Iron-on appliqués. Position the appliqué on fabric, right side up, and cover with a press cloth. Apply pressure with iron, using the heat setting and time recommended by manufacturer.

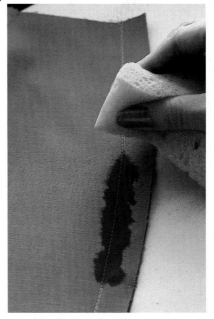

Dissolvable basting thread. To machine-baste, thread machine needle and bobbin with dissolvable thread, and set machine for longest stitch. To hand-baste, use 18" to 24" (46 to 61 cm) length to prevent tangling. Use water or steam pressing to dissolve thread.

Hook and loop tape. Use hook side on shoulder pads with matching loops on garment shoulder seam to make pads easy to detach. On sweater knits, use hook side of tape on shoulder pad only; it clings to knit fabric.

Three Uses for Liquid Fray Preventer

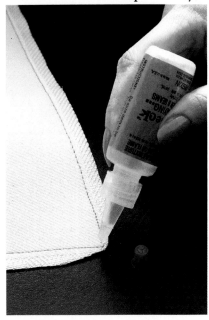

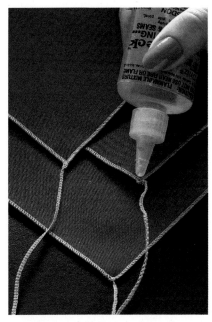

Reinforce edges that are clipped or trimmed close to a stitching line, using a single drop of fray preventer. After the liquid dries, the raw edge becomes firm and resists raveling.

Seal cut edges of machine-made buttonholes by coating them lightly with fray preventer. Test first on sample, because product can make fabric darker and stiffer. Remove excess with rubbing alcohol before it dries completely.

Finish row of overlock stitches by dabbing end with liquid fray preventer. Trim thread chains after liquid dries. Hasten drying with hand-held blow dryer.

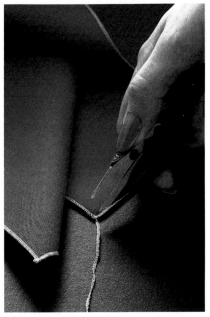

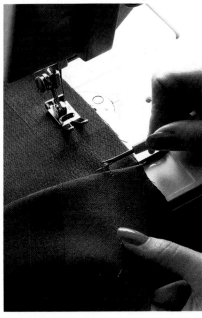

Button spacer. When sewing on buttons, adjust the movable U-shaped parts at end of gauge to make uniform thread shanks. Choose from three shank lengths, using thickness of one, two, or three parts at end of gauge.

Thread snips. Press spring-action blades between thumb and fingers to clip threads. Single hand motion takes less time than opening and closing scissor blades. To save even more time, tie thread snips on a ribbon around your neck.

Seam ripper. Insert prong of seam ripper under single stitches at 1" (2.5 cm) intervals to break stitch. Pull thread from other side of seam. To keep fabric taut, use presser foot as third hand to hold one end of seam. Pull edges gently apart to open seam. Do not slide ripper along seam.

Timesaving Pressing Aids

You can significantly reduce time spent pressing by assembling up-to-date pressing equipment, keeping it in good condition, and using it efficiently.

Pressing does not have to be done on a traditional ironing board. A convenient alternative is a small tabletop ironing board set up next to where you sew. This pressing surface is large enough for all but the final stages of most garments.

Another option is a professional-style press. It speeds construction pressing and the application of fusible products, because the pressing surface is larger than the soleplate of a household iron.

Pressing on curved surfaces, such as a seam roll (**1**) and tailor's ham (**2**), helps build in shape. A point presser (**3**), point turner (**4**), and pressing mitt (**5**) help you reach awkward areas.

Use an iron with a push-button steam feature (**6**), so you can concentrate extra moisture where and when needed during garment construction. Keep your iron clean. If fusing resins or web stain the soleplate, remove the stain with a special cleaner sold at notions counters. Cover the soleplate with a slip-on, perforated nonstick iron guard (**7**) so you can press on the right side of fabrics without a press cloth. Fusing products do not adhere to a nonstick surface.

Tips for Pressing

Do not stop to press after every sewing step. Group sewing and pressing into efficient batches.

Keep iron and other pressing equipment close to sewing machine to save steps.

Preheat iron so it is ready to use. Test iron temperature on fabric scraps to determine most appropriate setting.

Cut fusible interfacing and web on a table, not the ironing board. If scraps of fusible products are left on iron or pressing surface, they are hard to see and can become fused to your sewing project or iron.

Cover pressing surface with cloth when fusing; cloth keeps surface free of residue and stains.

Press (or finger press) before crossing two seams.

Press after, not before, understitching.

Directional press darts and tucks.

Slash darts in heavy fabrics, and press open on fold; do not press tip.

How to Save Time When Pressing

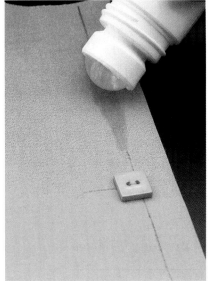

Fill clean roll-on deodorant bottle with water, and use to remove washable markings on right side of garment. Pressing over liquid markings permanently sets them.

Apply extra moisture to press crease-resistant fabrics. Cover seam with wet muslin strip, or use spray bottle, to press. White vinegar mixed with an equal amount of water can also be used to set creases; test first to see if it stains.

Press enclosed seams, such as collars and cuffs, before turning. Finger press short seams and darts with blunt end of point turner. Press over point turner for crisp edge. Press hems and cuffs lightly for soft creases.

Fusible Interfacings

Dozens of fusible interfacings are available, and all can be timesaving. They allow you to build shape and support into garments or to add a backing to home decorating projects with minimal effort.

Some fusible interfacings have been developed for a special use, such as shaping waistbands, adding crisp body to shirt collars and cuffs, or tailoring. Some are designed for a specific fabric, such as stretch knits or sheers. Manufacturers print guidelines on plastic interleaving and the ends of the bolts to help you purchase the right product. Follow their suggestions to simplify shopping.

Test-fuse a sample of interfacing and fabric to make sure you have made a good interfacing choice and to determine how much heat, pressure, moisture,

and time is required for sound bonding. Because you may require more than one type of interfacing in the same garment, it is convenient to have several fusible interfacing weights and types on hand and ready to use.

Fusible interfacings suit a wide variety of fabrics, but they should not be used on fabrics that are damaged by heat, pressure, and moisture. Fabrics that are unsuitable include rayon velvet, silks that water-spot or that cannot be preshrunk, heavily textured fabrics, and acetates. Also, it may not be satisfactory to use fusibles on fabrics that have a glazed surface or that have been treated for water repellency or stain resistance; these fabrics resist the penetration of fusing resins and prevent acceptable bonding.

How to Test-fuse a Sample

1) Cut fabric sample at least 6" (15 cm) square. Cut interfacing sample half that size. Place fabric wrong side up; place interfacing, with resin side down, on one side of square. Resin side either looks slightly shiny or has tiny raised dots. Cut small triangle of lightweight fabric, and slip under one corner of interfacing to provide unfused tab, which can be used later to check bonding.

2) Fuse, covering sample with nonstick iron soleplate or dampened press cloth. Use iron setting and time recommended by interfacing manufacturer. Use clock or watch with a second hand to measure the time accurately. Lean firmly on iron. It is necessary to bear down on iron to melt fusing resins completely and to force them into the woven or knitted structure of the fabric.

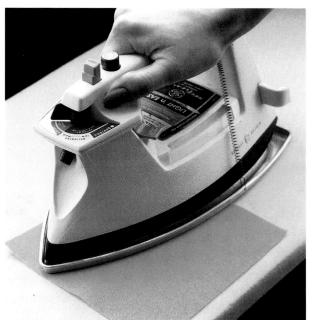

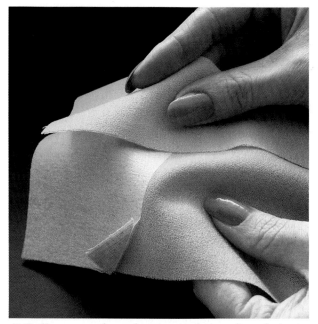

3) Turn sample over so fabric layer is right side up. Protect with nonstick soleplate or press cloth, and press thoroughly. Fusing resins are attracted to heat, so pressing on right side draws adhesive deeper into fabric structure for better bonding. Also, most iron heat is concentrated near steam vents. The second pressing helps fuse any areas not totally covered the first time. Let sample cool completely.

4) Pull corner tab, and try to peel away interfacing. Interfacing should feel permanently laminated to fashion fabric. Fold fabric over the interfacing to see if it creates the effect you desire. Handle sample to judge draping qualities. Look at right side to see if interfacing causes discoloration or if ridge shows through along edge. If desired, machine wash and dry sample to see how bond reacts to laundering.

Four Common Fusing Problems and Solutions

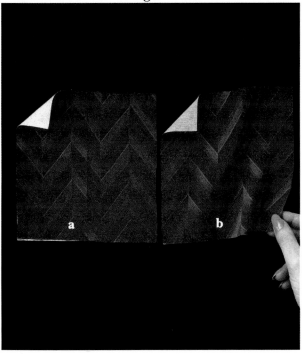

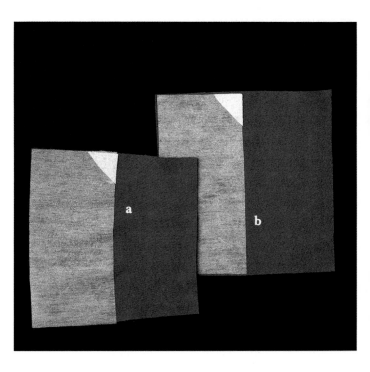

1) Interfacings show through to the right side of fabric **(a)**. Interfacing is too heavy. Test-fuse again, using a lighter weight interfacing **(b)**.

2) Fabric is puckered **(a)**. Heat and moisture used for fusing shrank fabric. Preshrink fabric to remove residual shrinkage; make another test sample **(b)**. Remember to preshrink all fabrics before fusing.

How to Apply Fusible Interfacing

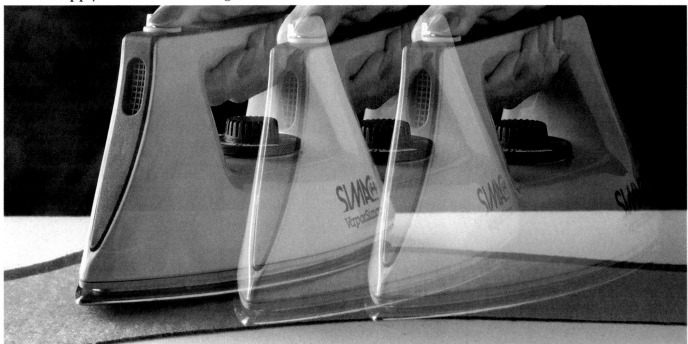

Trim entire seam allowance from interfacing if garment section will be topstitched or edgestitched; otherwise trim seam allowance to ⅛" (3 mm). Baste interfacing to garment section with tip of iron. Then permanently fuse, using the heat, pressure, moisture, and time used for test sample. Work from top down or from one side to the other, overlapping fused areas with the iron to be sure of complete coverage. If possible, work on surface large enough to hold entire garment section. As the first step in sewing, fuse interfacings to all garment sections.

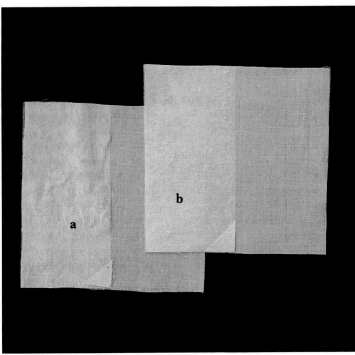

3) Interfacing bubbles **(a)**. Iron was too hot. Test-fuse again, using lower temperature setting **(b)**. You may have to increase fusing time when using lower temperature. Bubbling may occur after laundering the sample.

4) Interfacing peels off **(a)**. The iron was too cool. Test-fuse again, using higher temperature setting **(b)**. You may also have to bear down on iron more firmly to increase pressure.

Streamline application of fusible interfacings by using ironing press. Fuse several small garment sections at once, such as collar and cuffs. Or fuse large garment sections quickly, because pressing surface is considerably larger than soleplate of household iron. Ironing press is a worthwhile investment for household ironing or pressing and extensive sewing.

Save Time with Your Sewing Machine

Explore the capabilities of your sewing machine. Read the manual, and learn to use the built-in stitches and attachments in the accessory box. The more sewing you can accomplish by machine rather than by hand, the faster your sewing will progress.

Sewing machines are capable of far more than straight stitching. They can also baste, embroider, finish edges, make ruffles, apply bindings, sew on buttons, and more. Taking a class is one way to learn more about your machine's capabilities. Invest practice time until your machine's specialties become second nature to you and you will save time in the future.

The newest sewing machines use computerized electronics for easy operation and convenient stitch selection. Features vary among brands and models, but all allow you to store sequences of stitches in the memory of the machine. Therefore, you can push a button to produce a series of perfectly matched buttonholes or touch a control to have the machine automatically backstitch. There are a great number of built-in stitches, and you can program the machine to make limitless stitch combinations for creative decorative treatments.

Some state-of-the-art machines self-adjust for fabric thickness, automatically measure a button to create a buttonhole of the proper size, signal when the bobbin runs low on thread, and stitch sideways as well as forward and reverse to minimize the number of times you must pivot work. All these machines have fewer moving parts than older models, so they are lightweight, quiet, and easy to maintain.

Investigate the timesaving features available on new sewing machine models to determine whether you need to update your machine. To evaluate new machines, consider the sewing you usually do and the sewing you would like to do in the future. To appraise the cost realistically, divide the price of a new machine by the number of years you plan to use it. If a new sewing machine will help you sew more in less time and fits into your budget, it is a worthwhile expense.

Getting the Most from Built-in Stitches

Straight stitch is the most widely used stitch. In addition to sewing seams, hems, and zippers, straight stitches are useful for gathering, shirring, easing, quilting, applying trims, staystitching, topstitching, edgestitching, darning, and the timesaving stitch-in-the-ditch technique. Straight-stitch with a twin needle to form two closely spaced rows of topstitching with one pass. Vary the length of straight stitches for special purposes. Use short stitches to reinforce stress areas, to stitch curves and points accurately, and to secure the start and finish of seams without backstitching. Lengthen the stitch to make long, straight seams and hems or to ease and gather.

Sideways straight stitch allows you to stitch in confined areas, such as sleeves and legs, and to apply patches or appliqués without pivoting work.

Speed-basting stitch is an extra-long stitch formed under loose tension to make stitches easy to remove. Speed-baste to transfer pattern markings to the right side of garment sections and to prepare garments for try-on fittings. Clip threads between stitches to make quick tailor's tacks on a single layer.

Stretch straight stitch forms a strong, elastic stitch by moving the needle backward and forward in a predetermined pattern. Use it for durable crotch and underarm seams as well as stretchable seams on knits.

Zigzag stitch is the second most widely used stitch. Select it for stitching seams, finishing edges, attaching elastic and trims, darning, mending, quilting, hemming, sewing buttons, and joining butted edges. Adjust the stitch length and *bight* (sideways movement) for narrow, closely spaced stitches to make bar tacks, buttonholes, monograms, and other embroidery and decorative motifs.

Three-step zigzag stitch is similar to a standard zigzag stitch except three small stitches are formed with each swing of the needle. This stitch is more elastic than standard zigzag stitch, so it is especially suitable for seams and hems on stretch knits. It also stabilizes raw edges that tend to ravel or curl.

Blindstitch is used primarily for hemming apparel and home decorating projects, but can also be used to give zippers the look of hand-picked application and to couch decorative cords. Create a shell-stitched edge on lingerie or children's wear by blindstitching along a folded edge.

Overedge stitch sews ¼" (6 mm) seams and overcasts raw edges. Adjust to a short stitch length for overlock-style stitching for seams, reinforcing stressed garment areas, sewing stretch knits, finishing edges, and making decorative exposed seams on right side of garment. Adjust to a long stitch length for an open "M" stitch to couch cords or form scalloped edging.

Using Accessories & Attachments Efficiently

Do not let the names of machine accessories and attachments mislead you into thinking each performs just one sewing operation. Most are multipurpose. A ruffler, for example, can make pleats as well as gathers. Practice on scraps to become acquainted with the way the accessories and attachments work, and you will begin to recognize the possibilities.

The following are some of the most common machine accessories and attachments available. Consult a sewing machine dealer for information on what is available for the model you own.

Darning foot releases pressure on fabric so you manually control movement of fabric and path of stitches. Fabric must be stretched in embroidery hoop for stitching. Use for free-motion embroidery, darning, and mending.

Button sewing foot also holds hooks or eyes in place for machine application. Foot is most timesaving when you have a number of identical fasteners to apply.

Even Feed™ foot applies pickup pressure to help top layer of fabric pass underneath presser foot at same rate as bottom layer. An Even Feed™ foot is helpful for sewing without pins; keeping plaids and stripes matched; joining two types of fabrics; and seaming fabrics that tend to shift, such as velvet, and fabrics that tend to stick, such as vinyl.

Narrow hemming foot scrolls fabric to produce narrow, rolled hem about ⅛" (3 mm) deep. This hem is especially suitable for lingerie, ruffles, sheer fabrics, full skirts, and home decorating projects such as tablecloths, napkins, and dust ruffles. Also use foot to apply lace as you hem and to make enclosed seams on sheers.

Ruffler attachment has lever adjustment, so you can make perfectly even pleats or gathers for trims, apparel, and home decorating projects. Shorten the stitch length to make ruffle fuller; lengthen the stitch to make ruffle less full. You can also use attachment to make and apply a ruffle in one step.

Quilting foot has movable bar, which you can position as needed to help align topstitching parallel to an edge or another row of stitching. Short, open toes of quilting foot make fabric easy to maneuver when you sew floral, scroll, or other curved quilting or topstitching patterns.

Special-purpose foot has recessed channel on underside to allow thick stitches, such as satin stitching, to pass through without jamming. In addition to using this foot for decorative stitches, use it for applying narrow elastic or trims, such as soutache and middy braid.

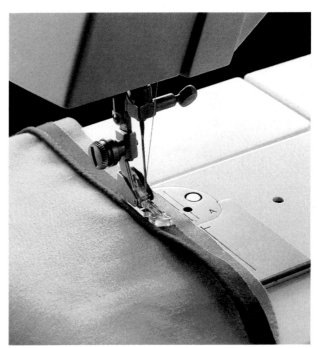

Zipper foot has single toe so you can stitch next to raised edges or seams, which have more bulk on one side than the other. Use foot for applying piping and cording and making bound buttonholes and welt pockets as well as for inserting zippers.

The Overlock Machine

An overlock machine, also called a serger, is a special-purpose sewing machine that supplements a conventional machine. It is similar to the speed-sewing equipment used by garment manufacturers. An overlock cuts sewing time considerably, because it trims and overcasts raw fabric edges as it sews the seam. In addition, it performs this three-in-one operation at high speed. Overlocks form 1,500 or more stitches a minute — about twice the rate of conventional sewing machines. As another benefit, all fabrics feed evenly so that even traditionally difficult-to-handle fabrics, such as slippery silks and thin sheers, will not take any extra sewing time.

Because of its unique capabilities, an overlock machine streamlines garment construction. It eliminates time-consuming steps and encourages efficient sewing habits such as flat construction, pinless sewing, and continuous seaming. It also dispenses with routines such as raising and lowering the presser foot, backstitching, and filling bobbins.

Functions & Parts

An overlock excels at making self-finished narrow seams, rolled hems, blindstitched hems, and overcast edge finishes. It is also the machine to choose for applying elastic, ribbing, ribbons, and lace. Use a conventional machine whenever straight or zigzag stitching is necessary, such as for topstitching, inserting a zipper, or making buttonholes.

Each overlock model makes a distinctive stitch and is identified by the number of threads it uses. The principal parts of an overlock machine are shown on a 4-thread model (opposite). Because it can also be adjusted to sew with three threads, it is called a 4/3-thread convertible overlock. There are two other commonly used models, a 3-thread and a 4/2-thread. Check the manufacturer's manual for specific information on the model you own.

Needles may be an industrial type with short or long shaft, or a standard type used on a conventional sewing machine. Use the needle specified for your machine. Industrial needles are stronger and last longer than conventional needles, but may be more expensive and less widely available. Change conventional needles frequently. Use the finest needle possible to avoid damaging the fabric. Size 11 (75) works well for most fabric weights.

Knives work like blades of scissors to trim the fabric for the stitch width selected. One knife is high-carbon steel and may last several years. The other knife is less durable and may require replacement three or four times annually. When knives seem dull, first clean them with alcohol; then reposition and tighten the screw. Test by sewing slowly. If a problem remains, replace the less durable knife and test again. As a last resort, replace the other knife.

Care & Maintenance

Because an overlock machine trims fabric as it sews, it creates more lint than a conventional machine and needs to be cleaned inside and out frequently. Use a lint brush or canned air to remove lint from the looper and throat plate area. Wipe off tension discs, needles, knives, and feed dog with alcohol.

To keep an overlock running smoothly and quietly, oil it often. Overlocks are lubricated by a wick system and can lose oil by gravity even when idle.

Overlock Thread

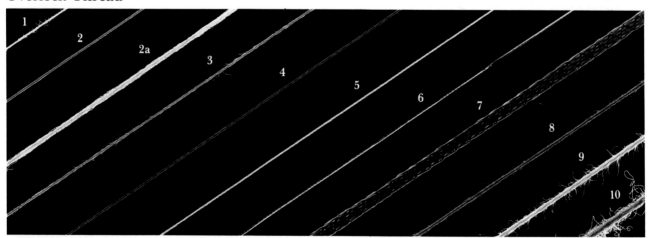

Thread that is fine and strong will perform best. Long-staple polyester (1) is a good, all-purpose choice; woolly nylon (2 and 2a) has exceptional strength and resilience. Cotton and cotton/polyester thread (3) also give satisfactory results but create more lint and may break with tighter tension adjustments and high speed. Decorative rayon (4), silk (5), and metallic (6) threads can be used for special effects, as can narrow ribbon (7), buttonhole twist (8), pearl cotton (9), and lightweight yarn (10).

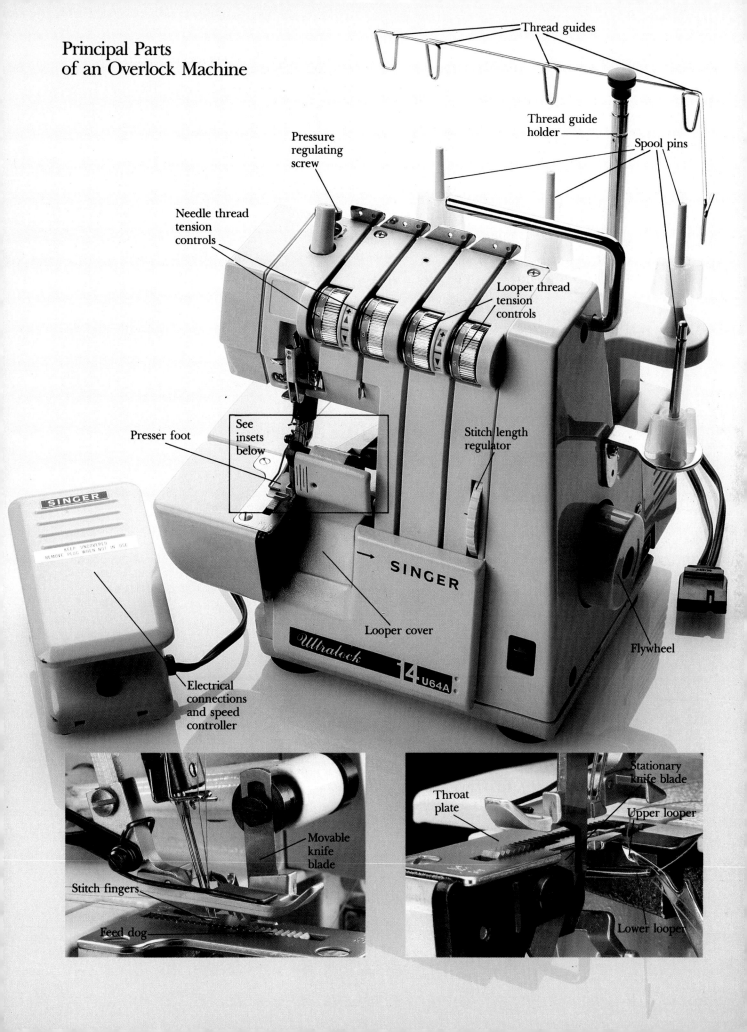

Principal Parts of an Overlock Machine

Thread guides

Thread guide holder

Spool pins

Pressure regulating screw

Needle thread tension controls

Looper thread tension controls

Stitch length regulator

Presser foot

See insets below

SINGER

KEEP UNCOVERED
REMOVE PLUG WHEN NOT IN USE

Looper cover

Flywheel

Electrical connections and speed controller

Ultralock 14 U64A

Movable knife blade

Stitch fingers

Feed dog

Throat plate

Stationary knife blade

Upper looper

Lower looper

Creating the Perfect Stitch

The tension controls on an overlock machine are actually stitch selectors. Each thread has its own tension control. Changing one or more tension settings affects the character of the stitch, because it changes how the threads loop together. With tension adjustments, the overlock can stitch a wide range of threads, fabrics, seams, hems, and decorative treatments.

A good way to become comfortable with overlock tension adjustments is to thread each looper and needle with a contrasting thread color. Copy the color code used for the machine's threading diagram. Make several stitch samples, tightening and loosening the tensions in sequence. You will see the effect of each tension adjustment and learn how to use the tension controls to create a balanced overlock stitch. Most of the stitch samples shown below and opposite were made on a 3-thread overlock; stitch samples made on other models look similar and are adjusted in the same way.

Correctly Balanced Tensions

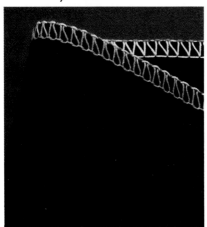  

3-thread stitch is formed by two loopers and one needle. Upper (orange) and lower (yellow) looper threads form neat, smooth chain at raw edge. Needle thread (green) forms flat stitches without puckers.

4/3-thread stitch is formed by two loopers and two needles. Upper (orange) and lower (yellow) looper threads chain neatly at raw edge. Both needle threads (blue, green) form flat stitches that interlock with looper threads.

4/2-thread stitch makes double row of stitches with two loopers and two needles. Left needle thread (blue) interlocks with lower looper thread (yellow) to make neat, pucker-free chainstitch. Upper looper thread (orange) and right needle thread (green) interlock over raw edge.

Common Tension Adjustments

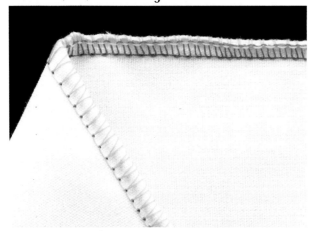 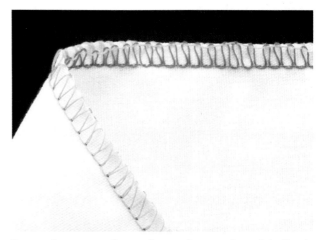

Upper looper too tight. Upper looper thread (orange) pulls lower looper thread (yellow) to top side of fabric. Loosen upper looper tension so threads interlock at raw edge.

Lower looper too loose. Lower looper thread (yellow) rides loosely on top of fabric. Tighten lower looper tension until stitches lie flat and smooth on fabric.

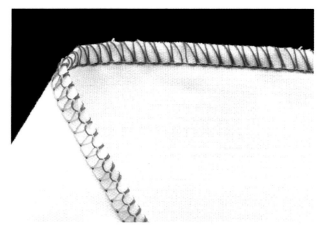

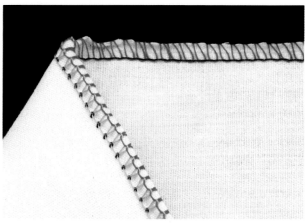

Upper looper too loose. Upper looper thread (orange) interlocks with lower looper thread (yellow) underneath fabric. Tighten upper looper tension so threads interlock at raw edge.

Lower looper too tight. Lower looper thread (yellow) pulls upper looper thread (orange), causing stitches to interlock under fabric. Loosen lower looper tension so threads interlock at raw edge.

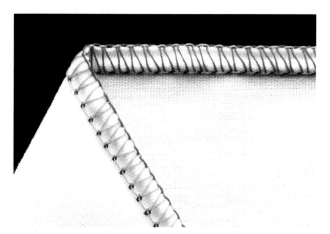

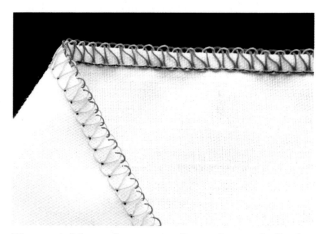

Upper and lower loopers too tight. Fabric bunches and puckers within stitches. Loosen upper and lower tensions until fabric relaxes.

Upper and lower loopers too loose. Lower (yellow) and upper (orange) looper threads interlock beyond raw edge and form loose loops. Tighten both looper tensions so stitches hug raw edge.

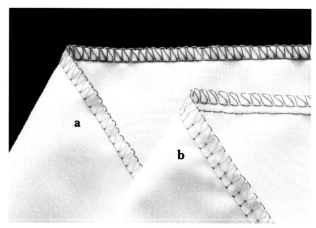

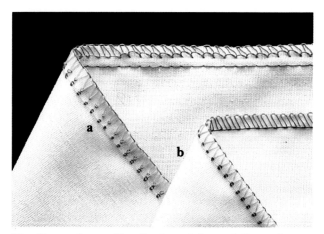

Needle too tight. Fabric puckers or draws up lengthwise when needle thread (green) is too tight **(a)**. Loosen needle tension until fabric relaxes. Test knits for thread breakage, loosening needle thread if necessary. On 4/3-thread machine **(b)**, adjust each needle thread (blue, green) individually.

Needle too loose. Needle thread (green) forms loose loops underneath fabric **(a)**. Tighten needle tension for flat, smooth stitches. On 4/3-thread serger **(b)**, adjust each needle thread (blue, green) individually.

Overlock Basics

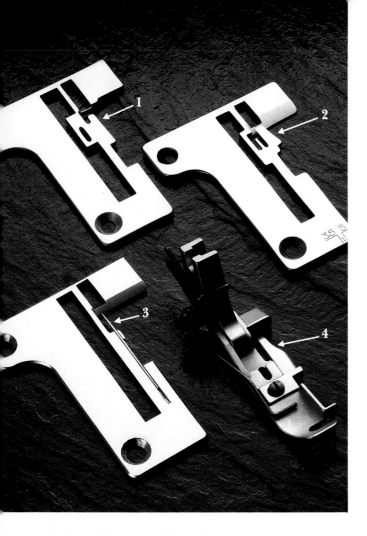

To begin overlock stitching, run the machine without fabric under the presser foot to create a chain of stitches about 2" (5 cm) long. A thread chain at the start and end of seams prevents stitches from raveling. Operating an overlock machine without fabric does not damage the machine or break threads, because stitches are formed on the stitch fingers (prongs).

The throat plate on most overlock machines has one **(1)** or two **(2)** stitch fingers. Stitches are formed around the stitch finger so that, with the correct tension, the width of the stitch finger determines the width of the stitch. A special throat plate with a narrow stitch finger **(3)** is used to sew a rolled hem or seam.

The presser foot may also contain a stitch finger **(4)**. Machines with this type of presser foot use a special presser foot for a rolled hem or seam.

How to Change Thread

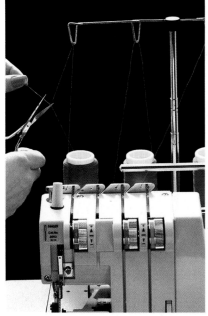

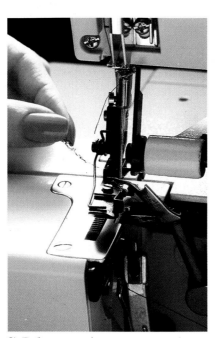

1) Cut each thread near cone, and remove cone. Tie new thread onto each thread in machine, using small overhand knot. Clip thread ends ½" (1.3 cm) from knot.

2) Release tensions, or set tension controls on 0. Cut needle thread in front of needle. Pull on tail chain to separate threads.

3) Pull threads one at a time through thread guides, upper looper, and lower looper. Pull needle thread until knot reaches needle eye. Cut off knot; thread needle with tweezers.

How to Clear the Stitch Fingers

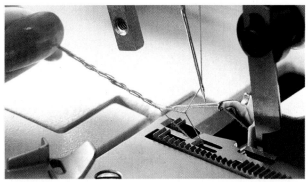

1) Raise presser foot. Turn flywheel to raise needle. Place left hand on thread chain behind presser foot. To slacken needle thread, pull it gently above last thread guide before needle. (Presser foot has been removed to show detail.)

2) Pull straight back on thread chain behind presser foot until threads separate and stitch fingers (prongs) of throat plate or presser foot are empty.

How to Start a Seam

1) Make thread chain. Stitch seam for one or two stitches. Raise presser foot; turn flywheel to lift needle. Clear stitch fingers. Run your fingers along thread chain to make it smooth. (Presser foot has been removed to show detail.)

2) Bring thread chain to the left, around and under presser foot. Place thread chain between needle and knife. Hold thread chain in position, and lower presser foot.

3) Stitch seam over thread chain for about 1" (2.5 cm); then swing thread chain to the right so it is trimmed off as you continue to stitch seam.

How to End a Seam

1) Stitch past end of seam by one stitch, and stop. Raise presser foot and needle to clear stitch fingers. (Presser foot has been removed to show detail.)

2) Turn seam over, and rotate it to align edge of seam with edge of knife. Lower presser foot. Turn flywheel to insert needle at end of seam and at left of edge the width of stitch.

3) Stitch over previous stitches for about 1" (2.5 cm). Stitch off edge, leaving thread chain. With scissors or serger knife, trim thread chain close to edge of seam.

How to Stitch Inside Corners and Slits

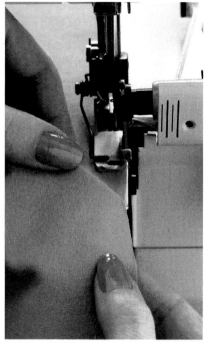

1) Finish seams of inside corners by aligning raw edge of fabric with knife of serger. Stitch, stopping before corner.

2) Fold the fabric to the left to straighten edge. This may create a tuck, which will not be stitched.

3) Resume stitching, holding fabric in straight line. Once past corner, fabric can be relaxed.

How to Stitch Curved Edges

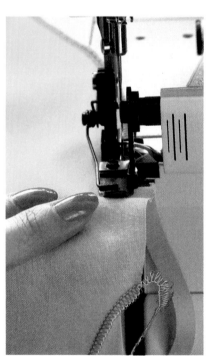

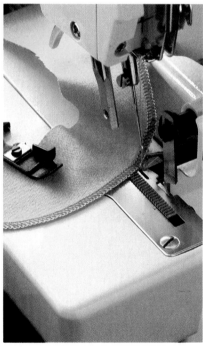

1) Begin cutting at an angle, until you reach the desired cutting or stitching line.

2) Guide fabric in front of presser foot so knives trim raw edge to curved shape. While stitching, watch knife, not needle.

3) Stop when stitches overlap previous stitches. Lift presser foot. Shift fabric so it is behind needle; stitch off edge to prevent gradual looping over edge of fabric. (Presser foot has been removed to show needle position.)

How to Stitch Outside Corners

1) Trim off seam allowance past corner for about 2" (5 cm). If making napkins, placemats, or similar projects, you can cut fabric to finished size and omit this step.

2) Sew one stitch past end of the corner, and stop. Raise presser foot and needle to clear stitch fingers and slacken needle thread slightly. (Presser foot has been removed to show needle position.)

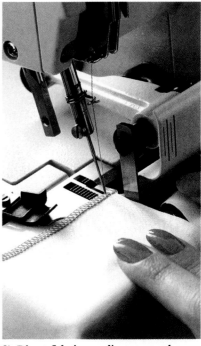

3) Pivot fabric to align raw edge of trimmed seam allowance with knife. Insert needle at serged edge. Lower presser foot, and continue stitching.

How to Remove Stitches

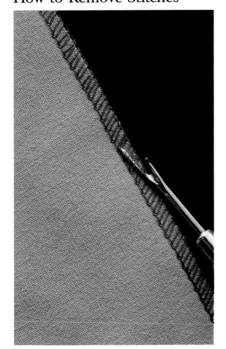

2-thread stitch. Cut threads by sliding seam ripper or blade of scissors under the stitches. Remove cut threads.

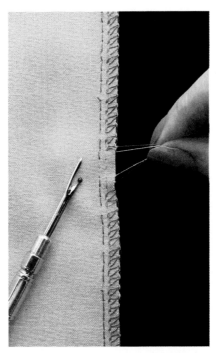

3-thread or 4/3-thread stitch. Clip needle threads every three or four stitches, working from upper side. Pull both looper threads straight out at edge. Remove cut threads.

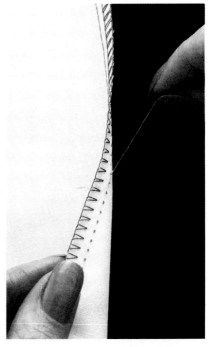

4/2-thread stitch. Working from under side, pull on looper thread to remove chainstitching. Remove overedging as described for 2-thread stitch, left.

Shortcut Techniques

Three Ways to Sew
the Same Pattern

The three dresses (right) are made from the same pattern, but each was made using a different method of construction. Standard, timesaving, and overlock techniques were used. Compare these techniques on pages 56-57.

Although you can successfully sew with the standard sewing methods shown on pattern instruction sheets, they are not the only methods to use. The pattern instructions usually do not feature timesaving tools, notions, and equipment, nor do they take into account your personal sewing style and favorite shortcuts. Most beginners follow pattern instructions to the letter. The more experience you have, the more natural it is to develop your own successful ways to put a garment together.

Feel free to deviate from pattern instructions by using alternative methods. If saving time is your priority, substitute shortcut techniques throughout, or combine timesaving and standard sewing techniques. You can also change the order of the sewing steps to take advantage of flat construction methods and to work on more than one garment section at a time for efficiency.

Standard pattern instructions also organize sewing steps into units that correspond to the major sections of a garment. For a dress, the units are the bodice, sleeves, and skirt. All sewing is completed on one unit before the next unit is begun.

To make any garment in the least amount of time, organize the sewing steps by task or type of activity; this keeps time-wasting interruptions to a minimum. *Fuse* all interfacings as a first construction step. Then *stitch,* working on all garment areas until you must stop to *press* what you have sewn. Continue stitching and pressing batches of work until the garment is completed. This method is different from standard sewing instructions, which direct you to complete one garment section before moving on to the next.

Also, practice the industrial-style techniques of continuous stitching and flat construction. For continuous stitching, line up the garment sections and feed one after another through the sewing machine without stopping. For flat construction, sew the final vertical seam in a section as the last step to make the sections easy to handle.

Standard sewing methods include continuous bound placket openings on cuffs; plain seams, pressed open and clean-finished; sew-in interfacings; and buttons sewn on by hand. These are traditional techniques given in pattern instructions and are familiar to most who sew.

Timesaving techniques streamline construction. For pattern layout, pockets are cut onto skirt, and front facing cut onto the bodice. Other shortcuts include fusible interfacings, topstitched hem, and buttons sewn on by machine. Placket opening is in the sleeve seam, and preformed cuffs on sleeves require fewer sewing steps. A timesaving fabric selection eliminates a need for a seam finish.

Overlock techniques cut down sewing time even further. Overlocked seams and rolled hems take minutes to sew and require no further raw edge finishing. Special overlock techniques are used for placket; back neck facing is eliminated, and one-step overlock method is used to attach elastic at waistline. Flat construction methods make garment sections easy to handle.

Compare Sewing Techniques

Seams & Seam Finishes | **Interfacing** | **Cuffs & Placket**

Conventional

Seams & Seam Finishes

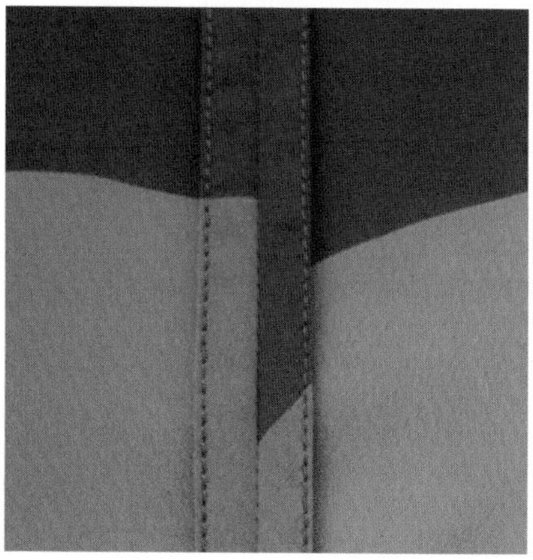

Plain seams, edges turned under and stitched.

Interfacing

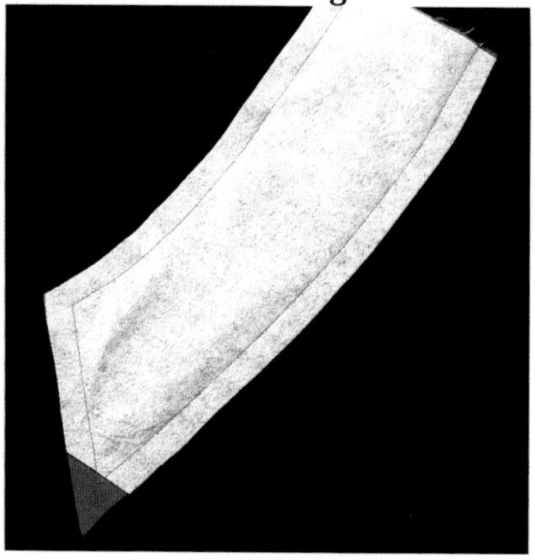

Sew-in interfacing following pattern instructions.

Cuffs & Placket

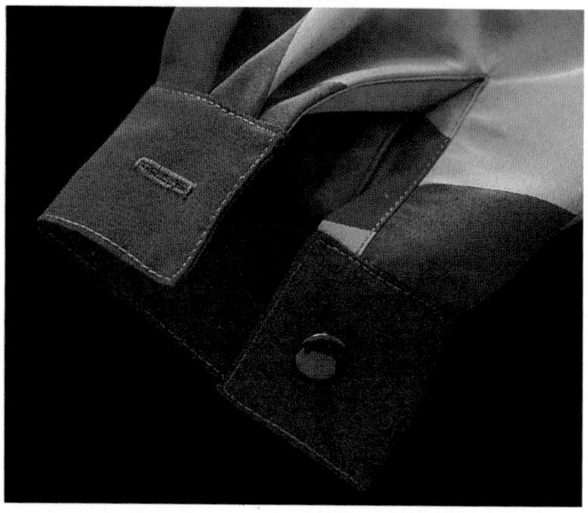

Continuous-bound placket opening; topstitched cuff following pattern instructions.

Timesaving

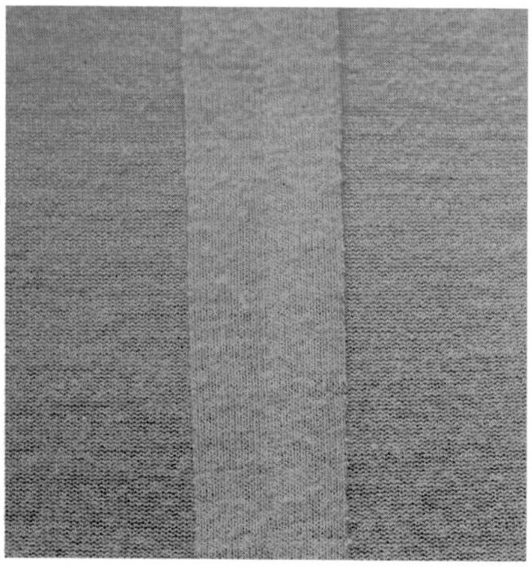

Plain seams on knit; no edge finish necessary.

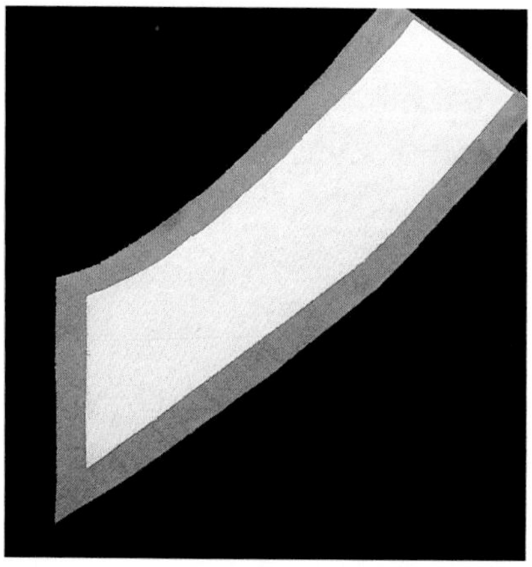

Fusible interfacing in front facing and collar (page 74).

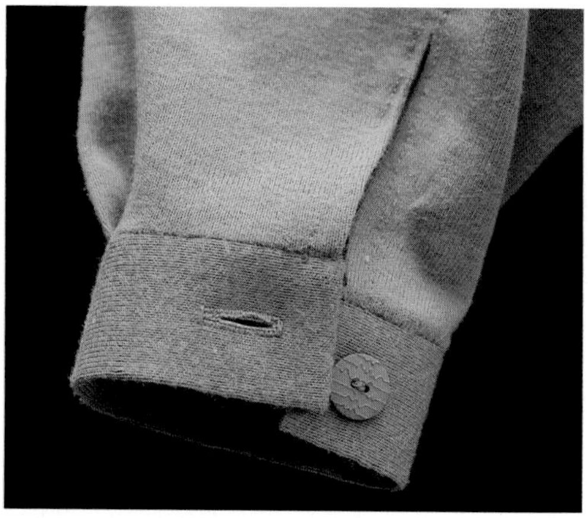

In-seam placket opening; preformed fusible interfacing in cuff (page 72).

Overlock

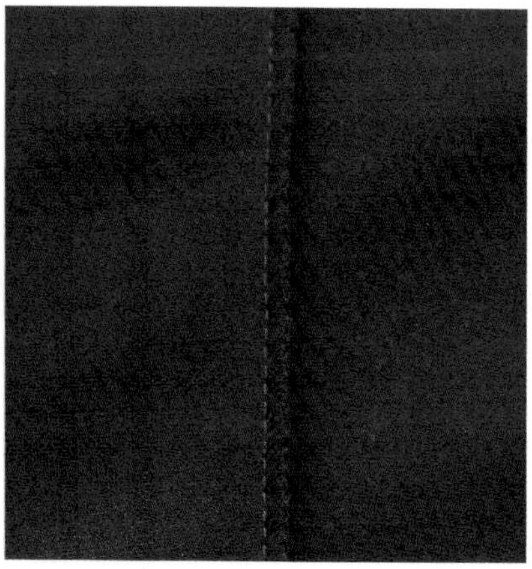

Overlocked 3-thread seams, stitched and finished in one step (page 68).

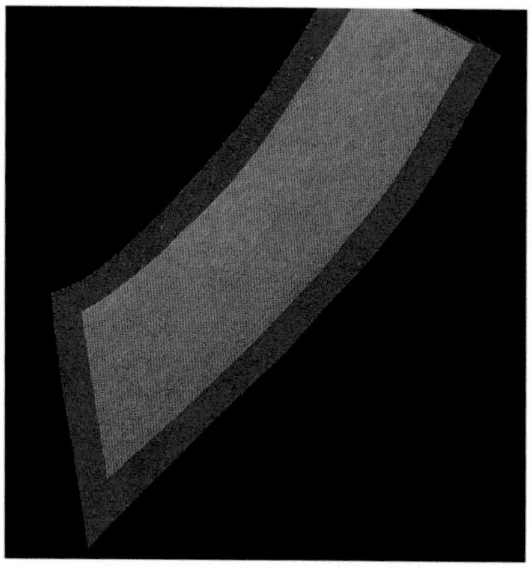

Fusible interfacing in front facing and collar (page 74).

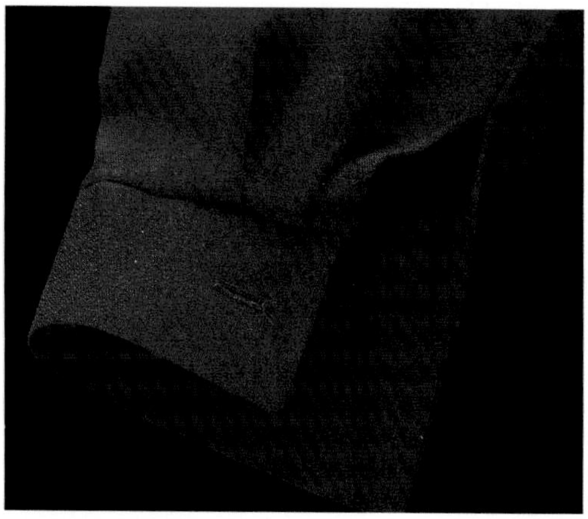

Overlocked slit placket; cuff attached with overlock seam (page 73).

Front Opening & Facings	**Waistline**	**Hem**

Facing understitched. Buttons and snaps sewn on by hand; machine-made buttonholes.

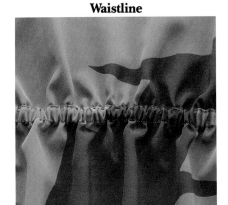

Elastic inserted in separate casing following pattern instructions.

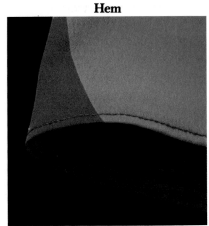

Narrow stitched hem, turned under and stitched again.

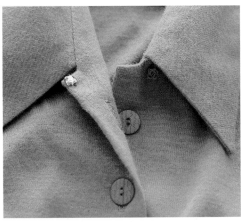

Facing cut in one with front (page 59). Buttons and snaps sewn on by machine (page 96); machine-made buttonholes.

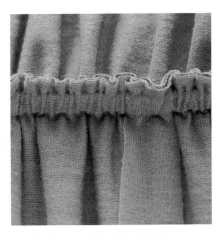

Elastic inserted in simplified casing; edgestitching and topstitching omitted.

Narrow hem with twin-needle topstitching (page 87).

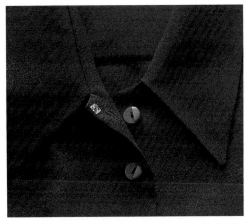

Back neck facing omitted and back neck seam overlocked (page 77). Buttons and snaps sewn on by conventional machine (page 96).

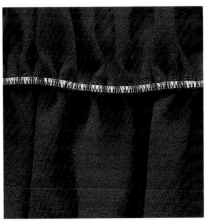

Elastic applied with overlock stitch (page 85).

Rolled hem, finished and trimmed in one step (page 91).

Timesaving Pattern Layouts

Pattern layout does not have to consume a large amount of time if you use some shortcuts. When using the same pattern pieces to cut more than one fabric, stack them into even layers and cut both at once. Because one pattern layout takes the place of two or more separate layouts, this technique can cut the layout and cutting time in half.

Fold fabric with right sides together for layout; after the fabric is cut, some edges, such as center back seams, will be in a ready-to-sew position. Do not take the time to make the crosswise ends grain-perfect unless you need square ends for cutting projects such as curtain panels. Simply line up the selvages, and hold them together. Let the fabric fall onto the cutting surface; smooth out any wrinkles toward the fabric fold.

Pin sparingly. Unless the fabric is slippery, one pin on the grainline arrow and one pin in each corner of the pattern piece should be sufficient. To cut layout time even further, use push pins or weights instead of straight pins to hold the pattern and fabric on the cutting surface.

Lay out straight-edged pattern pieces such as cuffs and waistbands with one side on the selvage. This provides a prefinished edge to speed construction.

To eliminate unnecessary seams, whenever possible lap adjoining garment sections that have straight edges. Side seam pockets can be lapped to front and back; a front facing can be lapped to the bodice pattern. This shortcut may require additional fabric and is suitable only if you are cutting the facings or pockets from self-fabric. On heavy or textured fabrics, use the standard method and cut separate pockets and facings from lightweight lining to reduce bulk.

Take Advantage of Selvages

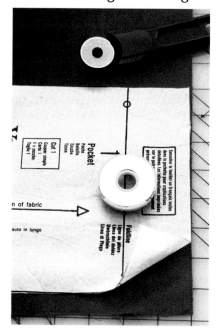

Align the straight edge of patch pocket self-facing on selvage. The selvage provides a prefinished edge and stabilizes and strengthens pocket opening.

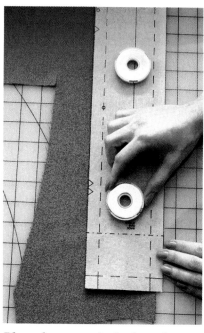

Place the unnotched edge of waistband ¼" (6 mm) from selvage to simplify construction. Edge does not need to be turned under, so bulk is eliminated. Finish from right side by topstitching or stitching in the ditch.

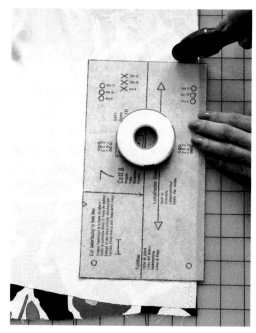

Lay out shirt cuff so the inside edge falls ¼" (6 mm) from the selvage. Self-facing requires no extra finishing steps beyond topstitching or stitching in the ditch from right side.

Layer Fabrics for Pattern Layout

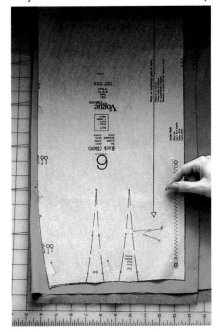

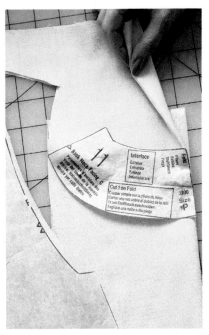

Stack lining and fashion fabric when they are the same width to cut out two layers at once. Push pins into cutting board through pattern and all layers of fabric. Trim excess lining hem allowances after cutting out pattern.

Cut two garments from one pattern at the same time. For easier handling, stack fabric that is slipperier or lighter in weight on top. Method requires that all fabrics be the same width.

Cut large pattern sections first; then slide interfacing underneath fabric before cutting collars, cuffs, and patch pockets that require interfacing. Trim fusible interfacings ⅛" (3 mm) from seamlines before application.

Lay Out Cut-on Pattern Sections

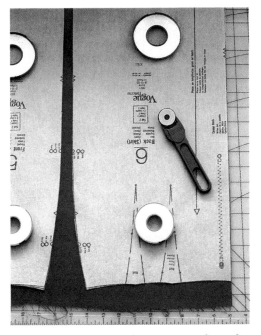

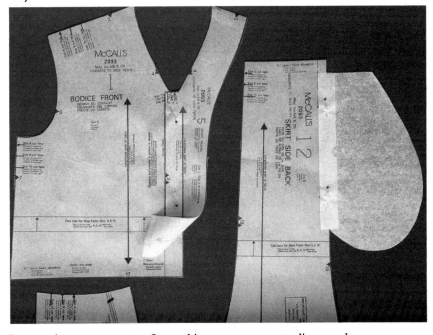

Position straight seams, such as the one at center back of bodice or skirt, with cutting line on selvages. No seam finish is needed. Clip the selvage of washable garments at intervals to prevent shrinkage.

Lap pocket pattern over front skirt pattern so seamlines and pattern markings match. Tape or pin in place. Trace pocket pattern to make duplicate, and lap over back skirt pattern. Lap front facing over front bodice pattern so seamlines and notches match. Tape or pin together, and handle as one pattern for layout. Extra fabric may be required for cut-on pattern layouts.

Cutting & Marking

Whether you use a rotary cutter or dressmaker shears to cut out a pattern, make sure the cutting edges are sharp and clean. Wipe the wheel or blades with rubbing alcohol to remove lint and residue, especially if you have recently used the cutting tool on synthetic fibers. Lint collects on cutting tools and makes them dull.

For easier handling, cut out the large pattern pieces first, then the small pieces. Ignore the notches; cut straight past them rather than taking the time to cut around them. As you cut out pattern sections, stack them to one side. Then mark all pattern sections at once, using the snip, pin and chalk, speed basting, pressing, or tape methods. Use more than one marking method within a garment if appropriate.

As you mark each section, remove all but one pin. Stack pattern and fabric layers in sewing order; the last section you anticipate sewing should be on the bottom. Detail areas with interfacings should be on top, so you are ready to fuse as the first sewing step.

How to Mark with Snips

Notches and dots. Clip into seam allowance to mark notches and other seamline markings, such as center front and back. Clip no more than ⅛" (3 mm) deep to avoid weakening seam allowance. Clip at top of double notch and center of triple notch to save time, unless notches designate front and back, such as notches at armholes.

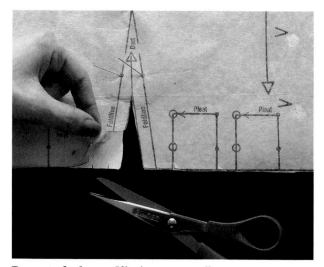

Darts and pleats. Clip into seam allowance to mark stitching lines at seamline end of darts. To sew, bring clips together and insert needle at clip. Mark point of dart with pin and chalk method, right. Mark fold and lap lines of pleats with similar clips.

How to Mark with Pin and Chalk

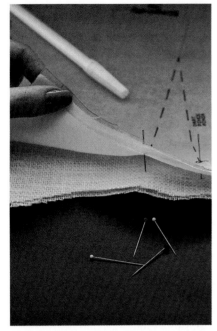

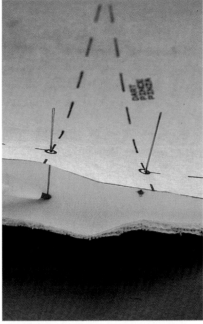

1) Stick pin straight down through pattern and both fabric layers at pattern symbol. Use straight pin with small head, or substitute hand sewing needle.

2) Lift pattern carefully off fabric. Mark top layer of fabric at pin with marking pen, pin, or chalk. On lightweight fabric, briefly hold washable marking pen in place to mark both layers at once.

3) Turn over fabric layers to mark bottom layer at pin. Separate fabric layers. Pin dart or pleat for immediate stitching.

How to Mark with Speed Basting, Pressing, and Tape

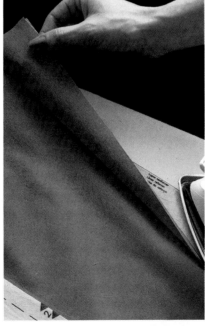

Speed basting. Set machine for tailor tacks, or use longest straight stitch and loose tension. Stitch through pattern and single fabric layer to mark placement lines for details such as pockets. Clip stitches at intervals to lift off pattern.

Pressing. Fold pattern and single layer of fabric along marking line for fold, tuck, or pleat. Press with dry iron to mark fabric. Press lightly to avoid leaving permanent crease, especially on synthetics.

Tape. Use peelable tape to mark wrong side of fabrics when right and wrong sides are difficult to distinguish at a glance. Place tape away from stitching areas.

Overlock Edge Finishes

Overlock machines make fast, neat raw edge finishes for pressed-open seams and machine or hand-sewn hems. Convert a 4/2-thread overlock machine for edge finishing by removing the left-hand needle and the lower looper thread; the machine will form a 2-thread overedge stitch without chainstitching. Convert a 4/3-thread overlock machine by removing one of the needles; overlocking with three threads

instead of four creates a less bulky edge finish and economizes on thread use. A 3-thread overlock machine can be used to finish raw edges without conversion. A 3/2-thread machine may be used as a 3-thread overedge or converted to 2-thread stitching.

Finish raw edges on an overlock machine either before or after sewing seams. Overlock after sewing

Four Ways to Use Overlock Raw Edge Finishes

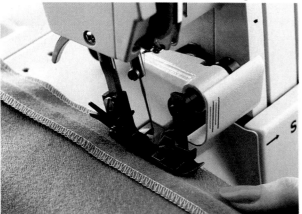

Finish seams by overlocking raw edges. Align raw edge of seam allowance with overlock knives to avoid trimming off too much seam allowance. Finish each seam allowance separately.

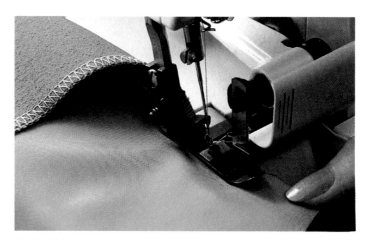

Underline garment section by edge-finishing before you sew. Place garment section and underlining with wrong sides together; finish raw edges of both layers in one step on overlock machine.

if cutting extra-wide seams for fitting purposes. You can use the trimming feature of the overlock machine to make all seams uniform. Overlock before sewing if working with a ravel-prone fabric, such as linen or a loose weave. You will not lose any of the seam allowance even if the fabric is handled extensively as you sew. Also overlock before sewing if underlining a garment section. Omit the time-consuming step of basting the layers together, and finish raw edges on both fabric layers at once.

Use a wide, long overlock stitch to avoid loading the raw edge with a concentration of thread. If you overdo it, the stitches can show through as ridges on the right side of the garment when you press.

Prevent raveling by edge-finishing loose weaves and bulky knits before you sew. Overedge each garment section immediately after layout and cutting to minimize seam allowance loss during construction.

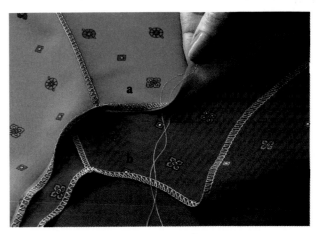

Prepare hems for stitching by overlocking raw edge. On shirttails (**a**) or other curved hems, overlock stitches automatically cup edge to ease in fullness. For shirts and blouses worn tucked in (**b**), overlock edge and omit hem for flat, smooth finish.

Seams

If you have selected fabric wisely, you can take advantage of several speedy seam techniques for stitching and finishing seams.

To avoid wasteful stops and starts, borrow industrial techniques. Instead of backstitching, begin and end seams with a short stitch; then lengthen the stitch to sew the seam. Use the longest stitch appropriate to the fabric. Also, line up garment sections, and sew continuously from one to the other without cutting threads between seams.

Practice pinless sewing; stopping to remove pins as you sew takes time. Develop the habit by gradually reducing the number of pins you use on seams. In the beginning, you will find short stretches, such as shoulder seams, easier to manipulate than longer seams. Children's garments, which have short seams throughout, are good practice projects.

To keep seams an even width, as you sew watch the edge of the presser foot or the edge of the fabric, not the needle. Guide the edge of the fabric against the seam markings on the throat plate, or use a topstitching guide or magnetic seam guide if you have trouble keeping seams even.

A pinked edge (1) is the simplest and most basic seam finish. Trim the raw edges after stitching the seam but before pressing so you can pink both edges at once. The three-step zigzag stitch (2) is another fast finish, although the stitches can make a ridge on delicate fabrics. For elasticity on stretch knits, use an overedge stitch (3) rather than the zigzag stitch. Use the tricot bound edge (4) on fabrics that tend to ravel or as a quick way to finish the inside of an unlined jacket. Tricot bias binding comes in precut, ready-to-use rolls.

Shorten Seam Sewing Time

Shorten stitch length at beginning and end of the seam instead of backstitching. Sew several short stitches; then lengthen the stitch to sew the seam. Short stitches lock securely and will not pull apart.

Stitch continuously from one garment section to another without cutting thread between sections. Sew with the fabric grain whenever possible, usually from bottom of section toward top.

Cut threads with thread snips, or hold scissors blades between thumb and first two fingers to cut with simple pickup motion.

How to Sew Seams without Pins

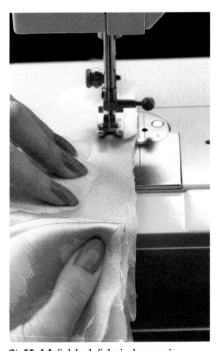

1) Match raw edges at beginning of seam. Select short stitch length, and sew several stitches. Then stop stitching, leaving needle in fabric and presser foot lowered.

2) Match raw edges at end of the seam, and hold them together in right hand. With left hand, match raw edges at 6" (15 cm) intervals along length of seam and fold into right hand.

3) Hold folded fabric layers in right hand, releasing folds one by one as left hand guides fabric toward presser foot to stitch seam. Fan out fingers of left hand to control fabric layers securely.

Shortcuts for Trimming and Reinforcing Seams

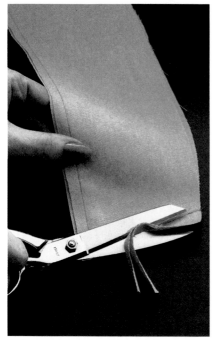

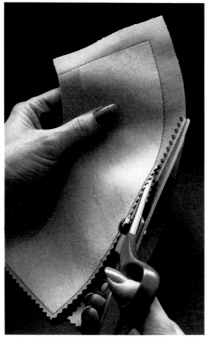

Trim and grade seam allowances in one step by holding scissors blades at an angle. Beveled edges reduce bulk of enclosed seams, such as collars and facings.

Use pinking shears to trim curved seam allowances instead of using separate trimming and clipping steps. Pinked edge spreads to release seam allowances on curve.

Add ¼" (6 mm) twill tape on seams that would otherwise need second row of reinforcement stitches, such as at armholes of tailored jackets, shoulder seams on knits, and underarm area of raglan sleeves.

How to Apply Tricot Bias Binding

1) Cut slit in plastic packaging, and draw binding through the slit to make a convenient dispenser. Binding tends to unroll and tangle unless stored this way.

2) Fold tricot binding lengthwise over seam edge. Stretch binding slightly as you stitch with straight stitch or medium-width zigzag. Binding automatically rolls over edge, so pinning is unnecessary.

3) Press with cool iron. High temperatures can melt tricot. Tricot binding is sheer enough to blend with fabric color and lightweight so it adds no bulk. This is a quick finish for unlined garments.

Overlock Seams

Overlock machines sew narrow seams with thread-bound edges. As the machine stitches, the knives automatically trim standard ⅝" (1.5 cm) seam allowances to ⅛" to ⅜" (3 mm to 1 cm), depending on the stitch width selected. Overlock seams are pressed to one side. An exception is a flatlock seam, a decorative overlock seam stitched on the right side of a garment. The trimmed raw edges of the flatlocked seam lie underneath the stitching line.

You can sew a garment completely on an overlock machine or use a combination of overlock and conventional seams within a garment. In either case, be certain of fit before you sew. After overlocking, there is little seam allowance left for adjustments if the garment is too tight.

Overlock machines feed fabrics evenly without shifting the layers, so you can usually sew without pins, basting, or other time-consuming preparation. Simply hold the layers in position and sew. If seams have shaped or eased areas, use small snips or a marking pen on the raw edges to indicate where layers must be matched. Sew from one set of marks to the next, holding the layers together in front of the presser foot as you sew.

If it is necessary to secure the fabric layers more firmly, use basting tape or glue stick. Apply tape or glue stick to the outer edges of garment sections cut with standard ⅝" (1.5 cm) seam allowances. The taped or glued area will be trimmed off as you sew. Avoid using pins, because they will damage the overlock knives.

Overlock seams work well on a wide range of fabrics, but you may prefer the security of wider seam allowances on loose weaves and other fragile fabrics. You may also prefer a standard seam for a crisp finish on tailored garments. In these cases, stitch seams on a conventional machine. Also stitch a conventional seam to preserve full seam allowances for a zipper insertion.

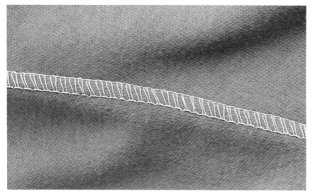

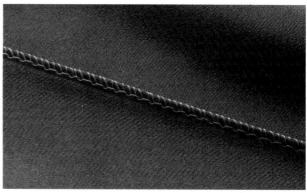

3-thread seam stretches for smooth finish on wovens or knits. This versatile seam is suitable for light to mediumweight blouse, dress, skirt, pants, and lingerie fabrics. It can also be used on two-way stretch knits for actionwear and swimwear.

3-thread rolled seam makes delicate hairline seam on sheers, thin silkies, and other lightweight fabrics. Stitch is created by tightening lower looper tension so raw edge rolls to underside. Adjust tensions and stitch length as for 3-thread rolled hem (page 91). For strong, flexible seam, 2 mm stitch length usually works well.

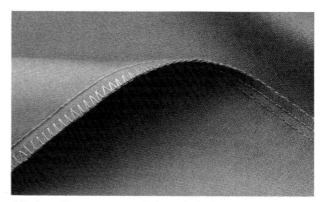

4/3-thread seam stretches less than 3-thread seam. Fourth thread adds extra row of stitches and makes seam more stable. This seam is especially practical for stable knits and woven garments subject to stress and wear.

4/2-thread seam uses a 2-thread chain and a 2-thread overedge to create widest overlock seam. Because this seam does not stretch, it is most useful for long, straight seams, such as those in draperies and jeans. It can also be used for pants styles other than jeans and for dresses and sleepwear.

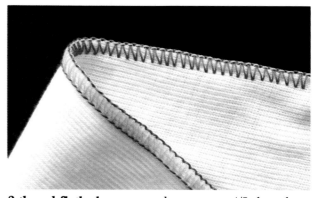

3-thread flatlock seam is used for decorative effects but is also functional because it reduces bulk. It can be sewn on 4/3 or 3/2-thread overlock models. Loosen needle tension and tighten lower looper tensions, so all threads interlock at raw edge. Upper looper may also need tighter tension.

2-thread flatlock seam can be sewn on 4/2-thread overlock model. Convert machine for 2-thread overedging by removing left needle and upper looper threads. Adjust tensions so stitches interlock at raw edge of fabric. Consult manual for adjustments.

How to Sew a Decorative Flatlock Seam

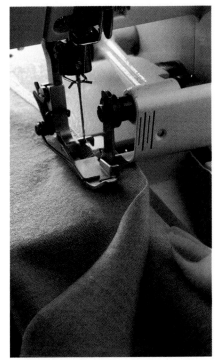 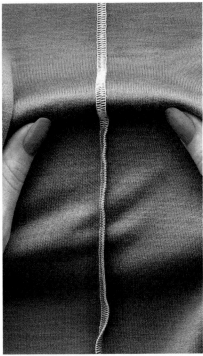 

1) Place fabric layers with *wrong* sides together. Stitch with needle on seamline so seam allowance is trimmed away.

2) Pull fabric layers apart to flatten seam. Raw edges of seam lie flat underneath looped threads. Seam is smooth and flat on right side.

3) Press, if desired. Trellis of stitch loops shows on right side. Ladder of horizontal stitches shows on wrong side.

Special Uses for Flatlock Seams

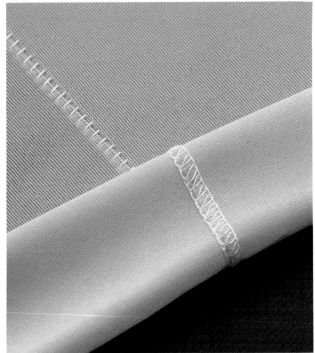 

Tricot is sewn with a 2-thread or 3-thread flatlock seam, with *right* sides together so ladder shows on right side of garment. This flat finish prevents lingerie seams from showing through as ridges on outer garments.

Sweater knit is sewn with a 2-thread or 3-thread flatlock seam, with *right* sides together so ladder shows on right side of garment. Ladder sinks into knit texture and makes seam almost invisible. Trellis on wrong side helps to secure yarn floats on patterned sweater knits.

Sleeves, Plackets & Cuffs

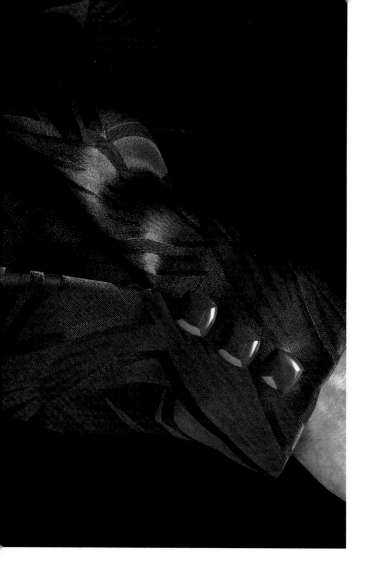

There are several timesaving alternatives to the standard cuff and placket opening in the sleeve. Use the sleeve seam as the placket opening to eliminate extra sewing steps. Or omit the opening and cuff altogether on slightly full or straight sleeves by finishing the lower edge with a pleat; on the right side, sew decorative buttons over the pleat.

A variation of the buttoned pleat can be used instead of a standard vent on a tailored jacket sleeve or as a substitute for a cuff and placket on a shirt sleeve. If omitting cuffs, lengthen the sleeve pattern to add an amount equal to the finished cuff depth plus 1½" (3.8 cm) hem allowance.

Use flat sewing techniques to set in shirt sleeves before sewing the underarm seam. Save time when inserting other types of set-in sleeves by using a combination of flat and circular construction methods. Use an assembly line technique for shaping a sleeve cap on an unthreaded sewing machine. No easestitching and few pins are required for a smooth, pucker-free sleeve cap, but it does take some finger manipulation. This method works best on crisp fabrics and on sleeve patterns with a minimum of ease, such as dropped shoulder and shirt sleeves.

How to Insert a Shirt Sleeve without Easestitching

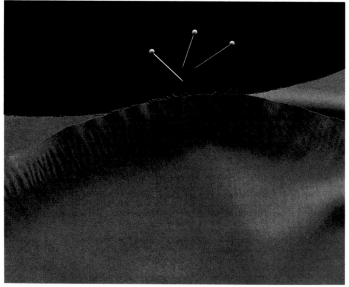

1) **Remove** thread from machine needle. Insert needle on seamline at one notch. Sew around sleeve cap from notch to notch, with index fingers firmly behind presser foot. Fabric will bunch up behind presser foot, causing sleeve cap to crimp. Use thumbs to guide the fabric under the presser foot.

2) **Pin** crimped sleeve cap at shoulder seam and notches, with right sides together. Sleeve cap is automatically crimped into rounded, eased shape.

How to Make a Pleated Sleeve Hem

1) **Try on** sleeve to determine excess sleeve width at wrist; pin-mark a pleat opposite the sleeve seam. Make sure opening is large enough for hand.

2) **Fold** sleeve from shoulder seam marking on sleeve cap to lower edge, wrong side out. Stitch on pin-marked line for 2" to 3" (5 to 7.5 cm) from lower edge.

3) **Center** stitching over pleat allowance to make box pleat. Press.

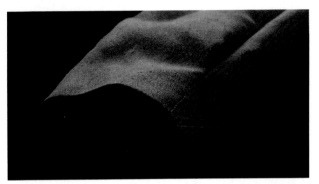

4) **Turn** hem up, and press. Finish raw edge of hem. To secure hem, stitch in the ditch of sleeve seam and pleat (page 87).

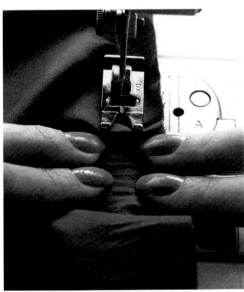

3) **Begin** stitching at notch with sleeve on top, guiding crimped sleeve cap into position with your fingers as you sew. Stop stitching at other notch.

4) **Stitch** underarm sleeve seam; then stitch bodice side seam. Use continuous stitching from one seam to the other. Press.

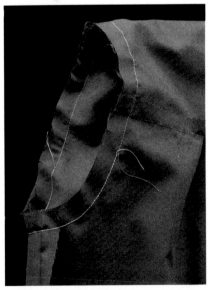

5) **Stitch** open portion of armhole seam closed. This sequence creates crisp break at sleeve underarm for quality finish, and sleeve fits well.

Three Timesaving Plackets

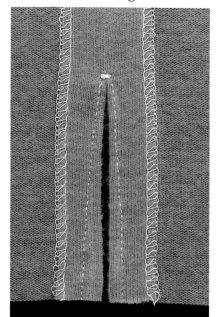

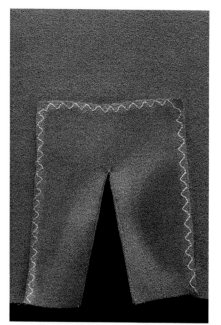

In-seam placket. Leave lower 3" (7.5 cm) of sleeve seam unstitched for placket opening. Overlock raw edges of opening, or turn under ¼" (6 mm) and press. Topstitch placket opening, adjusting machine for bar tack as you stitch across top of opening.

Faced placket. Cut rectangular placket facing 1" (2.5 cm) larger than placket opening. Overlock edges, or turn under ¼" (6 mm) and edgestitch. With right sides together, stitch facing to sleeve, following stitching line for placket slit. Cut slit, turn facing to wrong side, and press.

Continuous-bound placket with selvage. Cut 1" (2.5 cm) wide placket facing the length of placket opening, with one edge on selvage. Press crease ⅜" (1 cm) from the selvage. Stitch facing to opening in ¼" (6 mm) seam, with right sides together. Fold facing over seam; edgestitch selvage.

How to Make a Mock Vent (buttoned pleat method)

1) Try on finished sleeve, right side out, to pin-mark pleat. Make sure sleeve opening is large enough for hand to slip through.

2) Make a buttonhole in the pleat, stitching through all fabric layers. Sew button underneath.

Alternative method. Omit the buttonhole; sew one to three buttons through all fabric layers to hold pleat in place. This method is faster but closes pleat permanently.

How to Use Preformed Interfacing for In-seam Placket Cuffs

1) Interface cuff with preformed fusible interfacing. Fold and press cuff on perforation, pressing interfaced seam allowance to inside.

2) Stitch and trim short edges of cuff. Turn cuff right side out, and press. Press the placket seam allowance to the inside at lower edge of sleeve.

3) Pin non-interfaced side of cuff to wrong side of sleeve, before stitching sleeve seam. Ends of cuff extend slightly beyond sleeve. With cuff on top, attach to sleeve, stitching next to folded edge of cuff. Trim and grade seam allowance.

4) Turn cuff to right side. Topstitch close to pressed-under seam allowance. Stitch sleeve seam, leaving 3" (7.5 cm) opening. Finish as for in-seam placket, left.

How to Attach Cuffs with an Overlock Machine

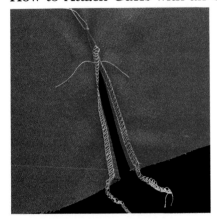

1) Overlock slit as for inside corners and slits (page 50). Fold right sides together, edges even; with conventional machine, stitch 1" (2.5 cm) dart at end of slit.

2) Make cuff. Pin both layers of cuff to right side of sleeve, folding edges of slit opening back over ends of cuff. Attach with overlock, stitching through all layers.

3) Turn cuff down to right side; fold and press edges of slit to inside. If necessary for crisp edge, fuse ¼" (6 mm) strip of fusible web under the folds of slit.

Collars & Facings

As you sew collars and facings, you will find that fusible interfacings and quick machine methods allow you to skip some standard sewing steps. These shortcuts do not show from the outside of the garment, so you economize on time, not on appearance.

Eliminate facing edge finishes by extending fusible interfacing to the edge. For this shortcut, trim fusible interfacing ½" (1.3 cm) on seam edges only. Do not trim the outer edge. Fuse, with the outer edges of the facing and interfacing matching. The fused interfacing seals the fabric along the outer edges.

Eliminate the back neckline facing on convertible collars. Instead of a facing, stitch the raw edges together with a zigzag or three-step zigzag.

Shortcut Convertible Collar without a Facing

1) Apply fusible interfacing to the undercollar and front facings, trimming and fusing as above. Make the collar. Staystitch neckline on seamline; clip into seam allowance every ½" (1.3 cm).

2) Pin collar to garment neckline at center back, shoulder seams, and center fronts. Fold each front facing around and over collar so right sides of facing and collar are together. Fold facing seam allowances under at shoulder seams. Stitch neckline seam. Trim corners diagonally.

How to Sew a Simple Facing

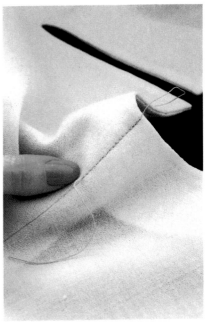

1) Stitch facing seams. Trim corners diagonally; then press seams open. Stitch facing to garment, right sides together, with garment on bottom. Sewing machine feed dog will ease garment to fit facing, so you do not need to staystitch.

2) Trim seam with pinking shears; then understitch facing to seam allowances. The understitching encourages facing to roll to inside of garment and speeds pressing.

3) Stitch in the ditch of each seam to secure facing without time-consuming hand tacking. Or use small square of fusible web between facing and seam allowances to hold facing in place.

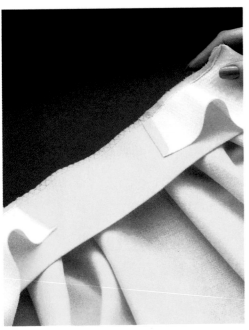

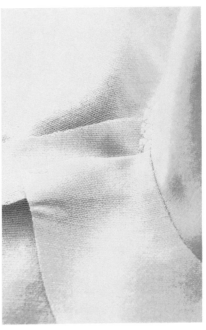

3) Finish the raw edges at back neckline between shoulder seams by zigzag-stitching all the layers together. If necessary, trim seam allowances evenly before stitching, and stitch close to raw edges so zigzag stitches overcast them.

4) Stitch through neckline seam allowance and garment between shoulder seams to prevent seam allowance from rolling to outside.

5) Use fine, closely spaced zigzag stitch to bar tack the facing seam allowance to the shoulder seam allowances on each side. Make bar tack about ¼" (6 mm) long.

Overlock Shortcuts for Collars

Use a fine overlock seam to sew collars made from sheer or thin fabrics. Either an enclosed hairline seam or an exposed rolled seam can be used. Both techniques save time, because you can skip the step of trimming the raw edges and clipping the curves.

Cut minutes from your sewing time by applying collars with the overlock machine. With overlock techniques, you can omit facings and eliminate the trimming, grading, and clipping because the overlock trims and overedges the seam in one step.

How to Overlock an Enclosed Seam

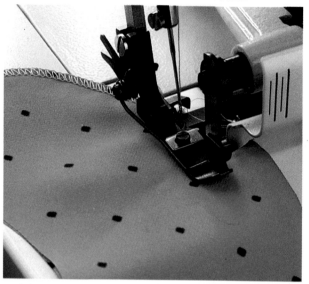

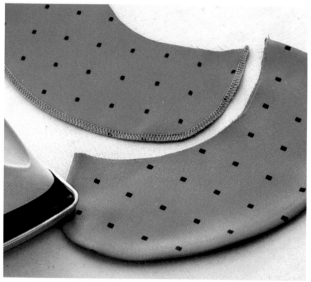

1) Stitch seam with right sides of collar together, trimming off seam allowance with overlock knives. Adjust machine for narrowest stitch width and 2 mm stitch length. Tighten looper tensions so stitches hug edge of curve.

2) Turn collar right side out. Fold outer edge along overlocked seam. Press edge with tip of iron to prevent seam imprint from showing through to right side. Overlocked stitches flex to ease in fullness along curved edges, so clipping is unnecessary.

How to Overlock an Exposed Rolled Seam

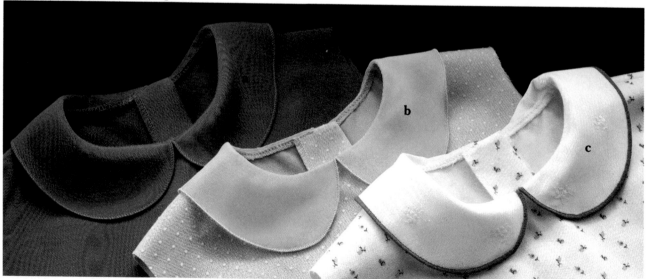

Adjust machine for fine, firm, rounded rolled hem, as on page 91. Stitch seam with *wrong* sides of collar together, trimming off entire seam allowance with overlock knives. Exposed stitches form decorative edging (a). Use one layer of fabric for collar, and overlock rolled edge for finest, most delicate finish on sheer or lightweight fabrics (b). Use buttonhole twist or woolly nylon thread to overlock rolled edge on collars on mediumweight fabrics. Contrasting thread color makes stitching look like piping trim (c).

How to Overlock a Flat Collar to a Neckline

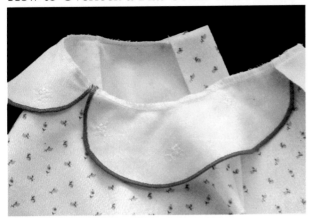

1) Place collar on garment, right sides up, matching markings. Fold facings back on foldline. Overlock neckline edge. Turn facings right side out; press.

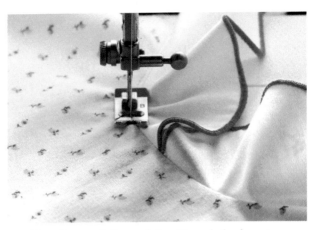

2) Lift collar, and from right side, stitch close to seamline, stitching through the garment and the seam allowance.

How to Overlock a Stand-up Collar to a Neckline

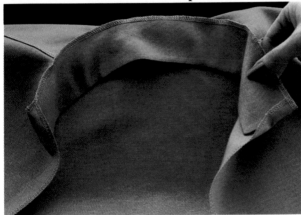

1) Place collar, wrong side up, on right side of garment; match markings. Fold seam allowances over collar. Overlock neckline edge, enclosing tail chains at beginning and end, as on page 49.

2) Turn seam allowances to inside of garment, and press. Press collar up. Use a centered zipper application for closure (page 94).

How to Overlock a Convertible Collar to a Neckline

1) Prepare collar and attach as for convertible collar, page 74, steps 1 and 2. Fold front facings back on foldline to partially cover collar. Overlock entire neckline edge, including facings.

2) Turn facings right side out, and press. Tack at shoulder seam.

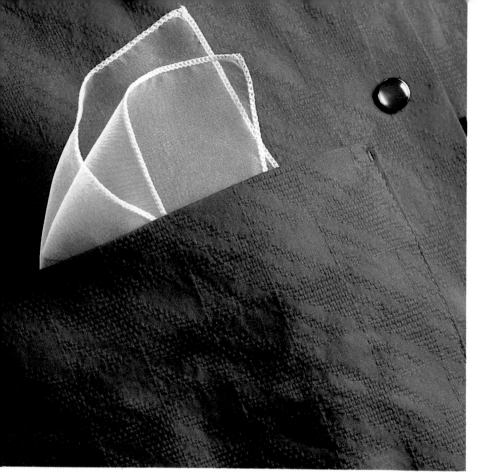

Pockets

It is easy to modify pockets on a pattern to make them faster to sew. Substitute patch pockets for more difficult welt pockets. Square the corners of curved patch pockets, or self-line pockets of a lightweight fabric to save sewing time. Cut side-seam pockets onto the major garment sections to eliminate a seam, or combine overlock and conventional stitching techniques to make the standard side seam pocket application go more quickly.

Speedy Self-lined Patch Pocket

1) Place top of pocket on crosswise fold of fabric. Cut two of fabric and one of interfacing for two pockets. On interfacing, trim seam allowance from outer edge; cut apart on fold for two pieces. Fuse to wrong side on one half of pockets.

2) Fold pocket in half, right sides together. Stitch pocket seam, leaving short opening on one side. To leave opening, raise presser foot and needle, and slide pocket past needle; continue stitching.

3) Trim diagonally across pocket corners. Press self-lining seam allowance toward self-lining. Trim and clip seams. Turn right side out through opening. Stitch pocket to garment as for unlined patch pocket, step 4, opposite.

Simple Unlined Patch Pocket

1) Cut fusible interfacing to fit pocket self-facing from foldline to cut edge. Trim seam allowance from short sides of interfacing. Fuse to self-facing, with outer edges even. Fusing seals edge so no edge finish is needed.

2) Cut 2" (5 cm) square template from cardboard. At each corner, position template on wrong side so its edges line up with pocket seamlines. Fold seam allowance diagonally across corner; then fold seam allowances back at sides and bottom of pocket to miter corners. Press.

3) Fold self-facing to wrong side of pocket. Press. Insert strip of fusible web between self-facing and pocket; fuse to secure self-facing.

4) Position pocket on garment with basting tape or fusible web (page 31). Stitch around edges of pocket; bar tack upper corners of pocket with zigzag stitches.

How to Sew Cut-on Side Seam Pockets

1) **Cut** lightweight, all-bias fusible interfacing from pocket pattern. Mark stitching line for pocket opening on interfacing. Trim ½" (1.3 cm) from pocket opening edge. Fuse to wrong side of front pocket extension.

2) **Staystitch** the pocket opening, stitching next to marked stitching line on the pocket extension. Staystitching adds reinforcement to pocket opening and helps prevent stretching.

3) **Stitch** garment side seam to dot, with garment front and back right sides together. Raise presser foot and needle, and slide pocket past needle; continue stitching from next dot to end of seam.

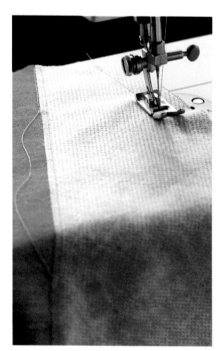

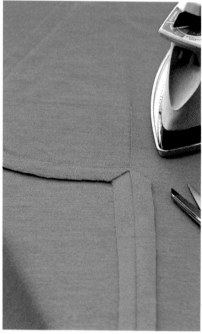

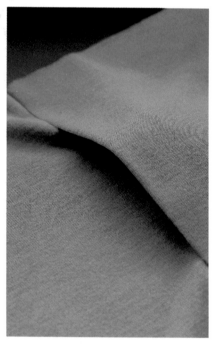

4) **Stitch** around pocket, ending at side seam.

5) **Clip** the garment back seam allowance at bottom of pocket. Fold the pocket toward front of garment. Press side seam open up to clip in seam allowance. Press pocket area.

6) **Finished pocket** looks like a continuation of garment side seam. Interfacing helps prevent gaping and weights pocket slightly for smooth drape.

How to Sew Side Seam Pockets (with overlock plus conventional stitching)

1) Overlock front pocket to garment front, and back pocket to garment back. Press seams toward pockets. Cut pockets from lining fabric when self-fabric cut-on pocket extensions would be too bulky.

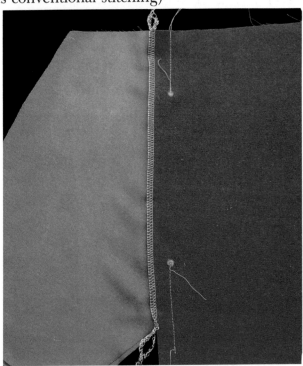

2) Use conventional machine to stitch garment side seam from about 3" (7.5 cm) below pocket opening to bottom of pocket opening, with right sides together. Stitch from top of pocket opening to upper edge of garment section.

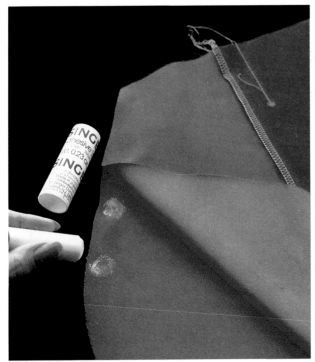

3) Baste pockets together with glue stick. This makes slippery lining fabrics easier to handle.

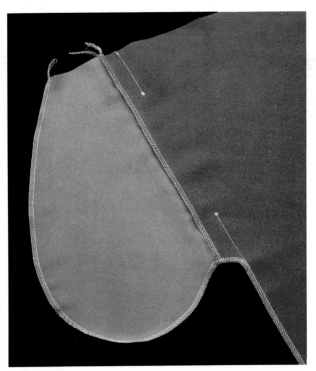

4) Overlock garment side seam, stitching continuously from lower edge up to straight stitching at bottom of pocket opening, then curving toward pocket to complete pocket seam. Press pocket and side seam toward front of garment.

Waistbands & Elasticized Casings

When you use precut notions such as fusible waistbanding and tricot bias strips, garment waistbands and elasticized casings take less time than standard methods. To adapt a pattern for precuts, omit the waistband or casing pattern during layout and cutting. Cut waistband after fusing the interfacing to the fabric; the interfacing actually becomes the waistband pattern. Use the garment itself as a guide for cutting a tricot casing; no pattern piece is necessary.

Two Types of Fusible Waistbanding

Single slot. Single row of perforated slots provides slightly off-center foldline for upper finished edge of waistband. Apply waistband with wider portion on inside of garment so you can catch the edge as you stitch from the outside. This waistbanding comes in two sizes for finished widths of 2" (5 cm) and 1¼" (3.2 cm). Because it does not extend interfacing into the seam allowances, it is not bulky and is especially suitable for medium to heavyweight fabrics.

Triple slot. Three rows of perforated slots provide foldline for seam allowances at both long edges plus center foldline. The center foldline corresponds to upper finished edge of waistband. This type of waistbanding comes in one size for finished width of 1¼" (3.2 cm). Because it extends interfacing into the seam allowances, it is especially suitable for lightweight fabrics and sheers.

Single Slot Waistbanding

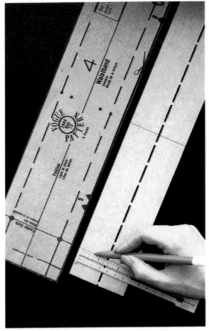

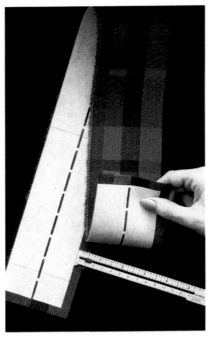

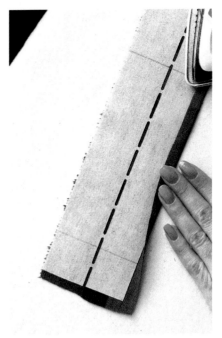

1) Cut waistbanding to length of waistband pattern minus seam allowances on short ends. Use pencil to transfer pattern markings such as center front, side seam, and notch symbols to interfacing.

2) Fuse interfacing to wrong side of fabric, with widest edge of interfacing on selvage. Cut out waistband ⅜" (1 cm) from edges of interfacing.

3) Press seam allowance over long edge of waistband. Firm edge of interfacing makes it easy to fold seam allowance evenly.

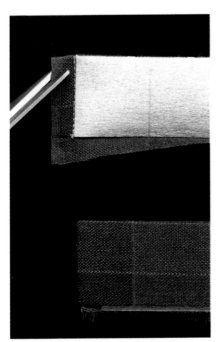

4) Fold waistband along perforated slots, with right sides together. Stitch seams at short ends with pressed seam allowance folded out of stitching area. Trim across corners. Trim seams to ¼" (6 mm). Turn right side out. Press.

5) Staystitch garment on waist seamline. Trim seam allowance in half. Position selvage edge of waistband on inside of garment with selvage extending ⅛" (3 mm) below staystitching. Position folded edge to cover staystitching on outside of garment. Pin.

6) Edgestitch lower edge of waistband along folded seam allowance, working with garment right side up. As you stitch, selvage on inside of waistband is automatically caught in seam.

Triple Slot Waistbanding

1) Cut waistbanding as for single slot banding, page 83, step 1. Fuse to wrong side of fabric. Cut around waistbanding. On long edge, press seam allowance up.

2) Pin waistband to garment, right sides together, matching pattern symbols. Stitch in perforations, and trim seam allowance.

3) Fold waistband on center perforation; stitch ends, and trim. Turn right side out, and press. Topstitch band in place.

Three-step Elastic Casing

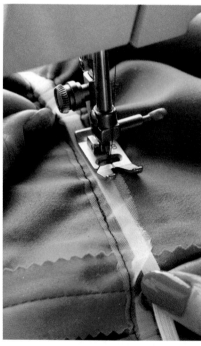

1) Stitch one long edge of precut tricot bias strip or bias tape to wrong side of garment on waistline.

2) Cut ¼" (6 mm) elastic long enough to fit snugly around your waist. Place elastic under tricot strip, and bar tack through all layers at one end of casing.

3) Stitch remaining long edge of tricot strip, encasing elastic. Adjust gathers behind presser foot as you sew to bring elastic to free end of casing. Finish this end of casing with bar tack through all layers.

How to Stitch a Casing or Mock Band

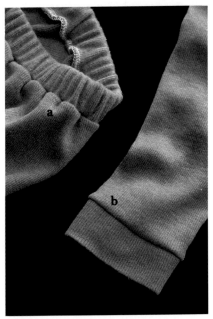

1) Set overlock for 3-thread stitch. Fold garment edge to allow for depth of casing or band desired, plus ¼" (6 mm) for tuck that forms. Fold garment edge back on itself, with raw edge extending ¼" (6 mm) past fold.

2) Align the garment edge under presser foot with fold next to inner edge of knife. Stitch on the fold so knife trims off ¼" (6 mm) extension without cutting into fold. For a casing, leave 2" (5 cm) opening for elastic insertion.

3) Pull edge down, and press. From right side, edge appears to have separately applied casing **(a)** or band **(b)**. From wrong side, you can see a tuck formed by stitching. Tuck creates simulated seam on right side.

How to Attach Elastic with Overlock

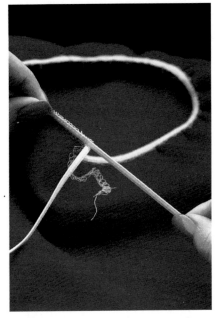

1) Use ⅛" (3 mm) oval elastic and a 3-thread overlock stitch. Position elastic between needle and knife, using guide on serger if available. Stitch onto seam allowance; without stretching elastic, stitch on seamline, overedging elastic and trimming seam allowance.

2) Pull elastic out of thread casing at beginning of stitching. Fold the elastic out of the way at the end of seam where ends of elastic meet. Stitch off the seam; cut elastic.

3) Pull up elastic to fit. Lap ends of elastic, and secure with small zigzag stitches.

Hems

Rely on machine stitches and precut strips of fusible web for fast, convenient hems. Machine-sewn and fusible hems were once considered appropriate only for children's clothing, rugged sportswear, and linings, but are now used on all types of garments. As a result, shortcut methods for hems can make your home-sewn garments look more professional than if you took the extra time to work by hand.

You can also save time by using efficient marking and measuring techniques. If the garment hangs evenly and the cut edge looks parallel to the floor,

mark the hemline with a single pin. Then measure from the cut edge to establish the hemline, rather than using the standard method of marking evenly from the floor.

To mark pants hems, use only four pins per leg. Turn up the hem at center front, center back, inseam, and side seam on each leg. Place a pin above the hem fold at each of these points. The pants hem will be ready to press when marked and measured this way. After pressing, trim the hem allowance to an even depth, judging the depth by eye.

Three Machine-sewn Hems

Choose machine-sewn hems for quick sewing that looks professional. For narrow hem (**1**), use narrow hemming foot, which automatically scrolls fabric into double fold. No pressing or pinning is required to create ⅛" (3 mm) finished hem. Hem is most suitable for light to mediumweight fabrics; straight edges are easier than curved edges. Topstitched hem (**2**) is suitable for hem of any width. Finish raw edge by pinking or zigzag-stitching before hemming. Add

second row of topstitching to prevent knits from curling or to add decorative accent. For a twin-needle topstitched hem (**3**), use double needle, zigzag throat plate, presser foot with wide opening, and regular straight-stitch machine setting. Two needle threads pick up one bobbin thread to make two perfectly spaced rows of topstitching at once. On wrong side, stitching resembles zigzag stitch.

Fast Fused Hem

1) Trim hem allowance to depth desired, but no narrower than 1" (2.5 cm) when using ¾" (2 cm) fusible web. Hem must extend slightly beyond web to avoid creating imprint on right side.

2) Position fusible web on hem allowance, with web ¼" (6 mm) below raw edge of hem. Clip web to make it lie flat if hem is curved. Fuse with paper backing in place.

3) Fold hem up. Fuse from inside of garment, overlapping previously fused area each time you reposition iron. Position iron below cut edge to prevent ridge from showing through to right side.

How to Blindstitch a Hem by Machine

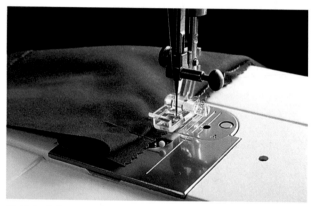

1) Fold hem up. Fold hem back to right side of fabric so cut edge extends past fold by ¼" (6 mm). Pin. Attach blindstitch hemming foot to machine, or use blindstitch hem guide with general-purpose foot. Adjust machine for blindstitching.

2) Stitch hem, using long stitch setting. Adjust needle position farther to right if necessary, so periodic zigzag stitch barely catches folded edge. The less the zigzag stitch bites into fold, the less conspicuous the stitch is on right side of garment.

How to Finish Pleats at the Hem

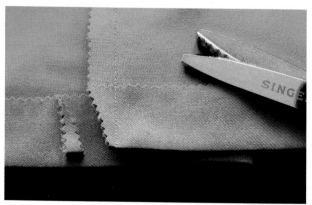

1) Leave seam open in hem area at back fold of pleat. Hem garment. Close opening at back fold after hemming; stitch seam through all layers.

2) Trim raw edges in hem area at angle. Seal with liquid fray preventer, or overlock edges together to reduce bulk and create crisp, sharp pleat fold.

Three Quick Ways to Interface Jacket or Coat Hems

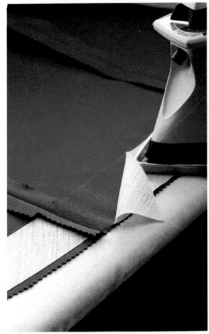

Fusible hair canvas. Cut crisp fusible interfacing to size of hem allowance. Cut interfacing on bias grain for smooth, flexible hem. Fuse interfacing between hem fold and raw edge of hem.

Sew-in hair canvas. Cut crisp interfacing on bias grain to size of hem allowance. Insert precut strip of ¾" (2 cm) fusible web between fabric and interfacing; fuse interfacing to hem allowance.

Precut fusible interfacing. Cut 1½" (3.8 cm) to fit between seams of hem allowance. Place perforated slots on hem fold with wider portion of interfacing on hem allowance. Fuse. This method is most suitable for straight hems.

Three Quick Ways to Secure Jacket or Coat Hems

Fuse. Fold up interfaced hem. Secure hem to seam allowances at sides and center back with 1" (2.5 cm) strip of precut fusible web.

Bar tack. Fold up interfaced hem. Bar tack hem by machine to all seam allowances. This method is especially suitable for bulky fabrics.

Stitch in the ditch. Fold up interfaced hem. Stitch in the ditch of all seams, sewing through all layers. No additional stitching is required to hold hem in place.

Overlock Hems

Overlock machines can hem two ways — rolled or blindstitched. On some overlock models, you must use a special throat plate, or a special throat plate and a special presser foot. All machines require adjusting the tensions and selecting stitch length. Consult the machine manual to learn what preparation is needed for your overlock machine.

Rolled hems (left) look like a satin-stitched edging or a hairline edging, depending on stitch length and tension adjustments. Select short stitch from 0 mm to 3 mm, the longer the stitch, the more softly the hem drapes. For example, 3 mm setting (1) creates soft, supple picot or scalloped edge; 2 mm setting (2) covers most fabric edges well and is not as stiff as the shorter stitch length; 1 mm setting (3) looks like satin stitching and has enough body to feel stiff; 0 mm setting (4) produces fine, firm edge.

When stitching a rolled hem, place the fabric right side up so the finished hem rolls under to the wrong side. Align the overlock knives with the hemline to trim the excess hem allowance as the stitches are formed. To provide a clear stitching guideline, mark the hemline with a marking pen with disappearing ink, or press a crease to mark the hem.

The rolled hem is a durable finish that looks fresh even after repeated launderings. For a decorative hem, use contrasting thread. Lustrous rayon or silk thread may also be used.

Blindstitched hem is similar to a flatlock seam. A ladder of stitches shows on the right side; a trellis of stitch loops covers the raw edge on the wrong side. Blindstiched hems are made with either two or three threads. Convert a 4/2-thread overlock model for hemming by removing the left-hand needle and upper looper thread. Convert a 4/3-thread model for hemming by removing the left-hand needle. A 3-thread model needs no needle conversion.

How to Blindstitch a Hem

3-Thread Rolled Hem

1) Fold hem up, then back on itself so raw edge extends past fold. Adjust overlock machine as for flatlock seam, page 68. Use blindhemming attachment if needed. Align hem under presser foot so needle barely catches fold. Overlock knives trim away excess hem allowance but should not cut into folded hem edge.

2) Pull hem down until stitches lie flat. Press. Ladder of stitches shows on right side. Blindstitched hem is most suitable for garments with straight or slightly curved edges and for stretch knits, because it also has some stretch.

Tighten lower looper (yellow) tension until upper looper thread (orange) rolls around to wrong side of fabric for rounded rolled hem. Tighten lower looper tension and loosen upper looper tension for flatter rolled hem. If puckers form, loosen needle tension slightly or hold fabric taut as you sew.

Overlock Shortcuts for Lingerie

Overlock machines make it easy to apply lace and elastic to garment edges, and they create a flat, nonbulky finish. The methods that follow are similar to the one-step methods used by garment manufacturers. No edge-trimming by hand is necessary. In addition to saving time, these techniques give garments a professional look.

When applying contrasting lace with the overlock, use a thread color to match the lace, not the garment. For seams, use the flatlock method shown for tricot on page 69.

How to Apply Lace Edging

1) Adjust overlock machine for 2-thread or 3-thread flatlock seam, as on page 68. Position straight edge of lace ¼" (6 mm) from edge of fabric, with *wrong* sides together.

2) Stitch seam, positioning straight edge of lace next to overlock knives so ¼" (6 mm) of fabric is trimmed off but lace remains intact.

Two Ways to Apply Lingerie Elastic

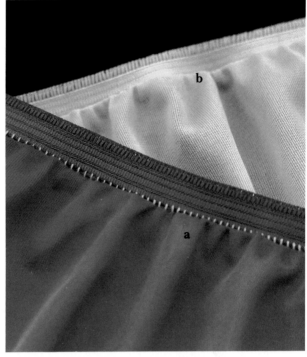

Flatlock method. Follow steps 1 to 3, below, for attaching lace edging, except place elastic and fabric with right sides together for flatlocking. Also, use longer stitch, and stretch elastic as you sew. Pull finished seam flat to open up stitches.

Hidden seam method. Stitch elastic to garment with 3-thread seam. Stitch with right sides together, and stretch elastic as you sew. This hidden seam method **(a)** hides seam on inside of garment but is slightly bulkier than flatlock method **(b)**.

3) Pull lace and fabric apart to open seam and make stitches lie flat. The stitch loops show on right side of garment (contrasting thread is used to show detail).

Alternative lace method. Stitch 3-thread or 4/3-thread overlock seam, positioning lace and fabric with right sides together. Allow raw edge of fabric to extend ¼" (6 mm) beyond straight edge of lace so raw edge is trimmed off as you sew. Press seam toward fabric.

Zippers, Buttons & Other Closures

The more often you can use machine methods to eliminate hand sewing, the faster you can sew garment closures. Choose from several timesaving methods for zipper insertions and buttons, including blindstitching by machine for a hand-picked look.

When inserting a lapped zipper with machine blindstitching, use a zipper that is 1" (2.5 cm) longer than the zipper opening so you do not have to stitch past the zipper tab. Your stitching will be straighter when the tab is not in the way, and the zipper can easily be cut to the correct length.

When sewing on buttons by machine, two-hole buttons are faster than buttons with four holes. Also, larger buttons are easier to handle than small ones.

How to Insert a Centered Zipper

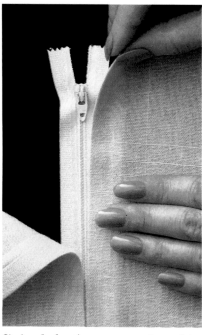

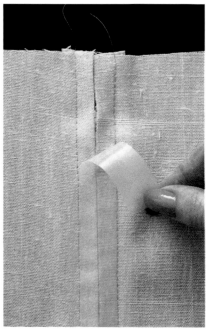

1) Stitch seam, leaving opening for zipper. Fold seam allowances under, and press. Fuse seam allowances down with ⅜" (1 cm) strip of fusible web.

2) Apply basting tape or glue stick on both sides of zipper coil. Place one side of seam on zipper so fold of seam allowance is centered over coil. Place other side of seam on zipper so folded edges meet.

3) Mark topstitching line ⅜" (1 cm) from folded edge. For an easy guide, center a strip of ¾" (2 cm) transparent tape over seamline on right side of garment. Stitch next to tape, using zipper foot.

How to Insert a Lapped Zipper

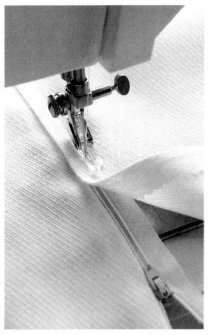

1) Stitch seam, leaving opening for zipper. Press under ⅝" (1.5 cm) seam allowances.

2) Open zipper. Place face down on back seam allowance, with zipper teeth on pressed seamline. Using zipper foot, stitch zipper to seam allowance. Close zipper, and fold seam allowance back.

3) Place basting tape on free side of zipper tape. Position pressed seam allowance on zipper so fold laps over zipper teeth. Topstitch across bottom of zipper and up basted side.

How to Insert a Lapped Zipper with Machine Blindstitching

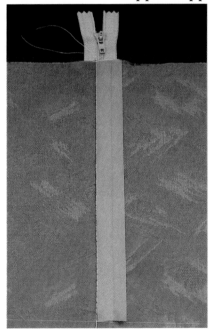

1) Use zipper that is 1" (2.5 cm) longer than the zipper opening. Prepare zipper as for lapped zipper, steps 1 to 3, above, except machine-baste lapping side of seam allowance instead of topstitching.

2) Fold lapped side of zipper on wrong side so seam allowance extends on right-hand side. Set machine for blindstitch. Using zipper foot, stitch along edge of zipper tape so periodic zigzag stitches pierce fold on lap.

3) Remove basting. Open zipper, and make bar tack across coils at top of garment. Cut off excess zipper tape. Press. From right side of garment, zipper looks similar to hand-picked zipper insertion.

How to Machine-attach Lining to a Zipper

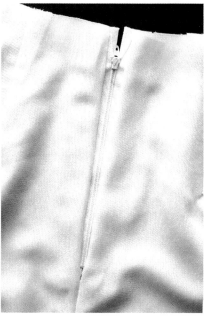

1) Stitch lining seam up to ½" (1.3 cm) from zipper opening. With *wrong* sides together, match lining and garment seams. Turn lining seam allowance under to match outer edge of zipper coil, and mark.

2) Match right side of lining at mark to seam allowance on wrong side of garment at zipper. Using zipper foot, stitch close to stitches used to insert zipper, tapering to full ⅝" (1.5 cm) lining seam allowance at bottom of zipper.

3) Match right side of lining to garment seam allowance on other side of zipper, and stitch as in step 2, left. Turn lining right side out, and smooth into position inside the garment.

How to Sew on Buttons, Hooks, Eyes, and Snaps by Machine

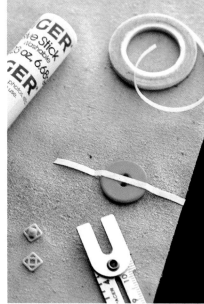

1) Position button, hook, eye, or snap in place with basting tape, glue stick, or transparent tape.

2) Use button foot on machine. Make several stitches in one hole to anchor thread. Adjust width of zigzag stitch to match spacing of holes in button.

3) Insert button spacer, toothpick, match, or sewing machine needle to create a shank for button. Make about five zigzag stitches; then make several stitches in one hole to anchor thread again. Cut threads; secure with liquid fray preventer.

To sew on snaps, adjust width of zigzag stitch to match holes in snap. Make several stitches in fabric to anchor snap.

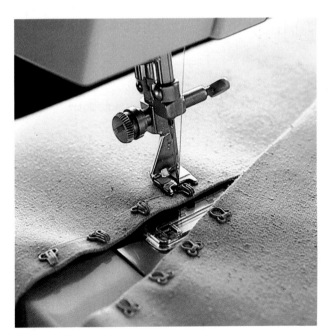

To sew on hooks and eyes, make about five zigzag stitches to sew over loop. Without cutting threads, move to next hook or eye. Then, clip threads close to hook, pull to wrong side. Secure thread ends with liquid fray preventer.

Home Decorating

Timesaving Fabrics for Home Decorating

Whether you are planning a large or small home decorating project, the choice of fabric can save you time in the long run. When looking for fabrics that are timesaving, use these general guidelines.

Prints bring style and the impression of detailing to quick sewing projects. They also provide a built-in color scheme for attractive room settings, hide any imperfect stitches, and show soil or wear less quickly than plain fabrics. Choose allover or small-scale prints rather than larger motifs that must be matched at the seams, centered, or balanced, and you will save fabric as well as time.

Coordinated prints give you a custom look quickly. These fabrics may have coordinated borders or a companion print, such as a stripe, that can be cut apart for trims, tiebacks, and ruffles. Specialty groups include decorative panels that look like handcrafted patchwork or appliqué for shortcut wall hangings and pillows. There are also preprints designed for easy-to-make home accessories, such as kitchen appliance covers, placemat and napkin sets, holiday accents, and nursery items.

Dull or matte finish fabrics absorb rather than reflect light; therefore, they do not require the perfection in sewing or draping needed for fabrics with luster or sheen.

Wide fabrics are best for large projects, such as window treatments, bed coverings, and tablecloths; the wider the fabric, the fewer the seams that are needed. Most home decorating fabrics are at least 54" (140 cm) wide to keep seams to the minimum, but some sheers are 110" (280 cm) or wider so you can eliminate seams entirely. For seamless window treatments, choose fabric wide enough to make headings and lower hems on the selvage edges so the lengthwise fabric grain runs across the window.

Flat bed sheets come in generous sizes that are often large enough for seamless projects. In addition, many sheet styles have borders or applied trims that can be used as prefinished project edges or cut apart to make small items, such as tiebacks.

Reversible fabric, which has no apparent right or wrong side, allows you to eliminate linings and backings. Both fabric faces are attractive on many sheers, jacquard weaves, synthetic suedes, and woven plaids. Create a reversible fabric by using two fabrics back to back. Glue, fuse, or machine-baste wrong sides together.

Lace is suitable for many decorating projects; it does not ravel or require hems or linings. Take advantage of lace border designs by using them as ready-made edges. For window treatments, choose lace that has one edge prefinished as a border and the other prefinished with openings for a curtain rod.

Knits are usually wide enough to minimize seaming; they drape well and may not require hemming. Use velour for pillows, and lightweight tricot for full sheer curtains.

Plaids and stripes have built-in timesaving features. For cutting, measuring, and marking, the lines of a woven plaid or stripe are always on a straight grain. Check to be sure that a printed geometric is printed on-grain or it will be difficult to work with.

Notions & Equipment

Fusible web saves time when used to apply trim or make hems as well as to anchor seam allowances inside a casing for easy curtain rod insertion.

Glue stick is a fast way to position trims, hems, backings, and linings for stitching.

Liquid fray preventer seals the exposed and cut edges on non-sew slits cut into curtains or valances for inserting a rod or brackets.

Overlock machine makes neat, fast hems and edge finishes on ruffles, shades, tablecloths, runners, placemats, and napkins. Also use the overlock machine to sew sheer fabrics without puckers and to sew long, straight seams on curtains, draperies, or bed coverings in minutes.

Rotary cutter is ideal for cutting straight pieces, such as ties, ruffles, bindings, and trimming strips.

Bias tape maker uniformly folds the raw edges of fabric strips as you press. Use it for bias binding, curtain tabs, decorative tapes, and custom band trims. Tape makers come in four sizes to make folded strips ½", ¾", 1", or 2" (12, 18, 25, or 50 mm).

Fabric adhesive, such as craft or white glue, can be used to anchor a shade hem to a lining or to close an opening left for turning a project right side out.

Tapes with self-styling cords are stitched flat to fabric and pulled to shirr, smock, pleat, or fold fabric automatically. Tape is a fast, easy way to make decorative headings on curtains, draperies, valances, and dust ruffles. Ring tape and shade tape are other self-styling tapes. Ring tape has plastic rings sewn at 6" (15 cm) intervals; shade tape has cord tacked loosely at intervals. Both can be used to form swagged hems quickly.

Timesaving Seams

Selvage eliminates need for edge finish. Place as many straight seams as possible at selvage edges of fabric. For all home decorating projects, use ½" (1.3 cm) seam allowances unless stated otherwise.

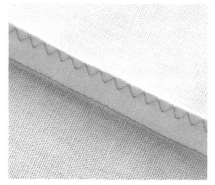

Zigzag stitching holds the seam allowances together. Technique is similar to overedging but does not require trimming step. Position stitches as close to raw edges as possible. Press to one side.

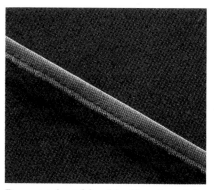

Precut tricot bias binding is quick edge finish. Sheer, lightweight binding is especially suitable for ravel-prone, textured, and thick fabrics. Bind seam allowances together; press to one side.

4-thread overlock seam is durable, nonstretch, self-finished seam. It has wide application for home decorator sewing, especially on long, straight seams.

3-thread overlock seam is suitable alternative for 4-thread seam in most situations; use conventional sewing machine to add row of straight stitches to reinforce and prevent stretching.

2-thread overlock stitch is fast, neat technique for finishing raw edges of plain seams. Overlock raw edges either before or after stitching seam.

Timesaving Gathers

Zigzag over strong, thin cord to gather with single row of stitches. Use topstitching thread, dental floss, string, or crochet cotton. Do not let stitches catch cord.

Divide project edge and edge to be gathered into fourths, and mark. For large projects, divide into eight or more parts. Pin edges together at markings. Pull up gathering cord between marks.

Ruffler gathers fabric evenly, and is especially useful for dust ruffles and ruffles for tablecloths and curtains. Adjust fullness on ruffler to suit fabric and use of ruffle.

Timesaving Hems

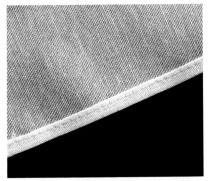

Narrow hem is suitable for ruffles, tablecloths, placemats, and napkins. Use narrow hemming foot to fold fabric automatically without pressing or pinning. Foot creates uniform ⅛" (3 mm) hem.

Double side hem 1" (2.5 cm) deep is standard for window treatments. Press under scant 1" (2.5 cm); then fold under another 1" (2.5 cm), and press. Topstitch, blindstitch, or fuse.

Double bottom hem 2" to 6" (5 to 15 cm) deep is standard for window treatments. The longer the panel and lighter weight the fabric, the deeper the hem. Fold, press, and finish as for side hem, left.

Topstitched hem is fast way to hem on conventional machine. Use 8 to 10 stitches per inch (3.5 to 3 mm); stitch next to folded hem edge. Topstitching is durable finish, but line of stitching shows on right side.

Blindstitched hem is nearly inconspicuous from right side and looks like hand-sewn hem. Use blindstitch machine setting and blindstitch foot or guide. Position hem edge so zigzag stitch takes tiny bite into fabric panel.

Fused hem creates firm, crisp hem without stitches. Use precut fusible web strips. Position web ⅛" (3 mm) beneath folded hem edge; fuse, following package instructions. To prevent imprint on right side, do not press directly on folded edge.

Timesaving Alternatives to Hems

Rolled edge sewn with 3-thread or 2-thread overlock stitch is durable and neat. Use it on tablecloths, napkins, and ruffles that would otherwise require narrow hem. Contrasting thread can be used for a decorative detail.

Satin edge sewn with short, narrow 3-thread or 2-thread overlock stitch can take place of narrow hem or rolled edge. This method, good on textured fabrics, is less bulky than rolled edge. Use woolly nylon thread for good coverage.

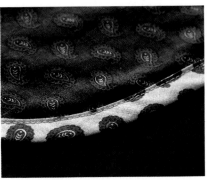

Bias bound edge is useful on curved edges or on heavy or quilted fabrics that are too bulky to hem. Use purchased binding, or make your own using tape maker pressing aid.

Flip Top Curtains

To create this one-piece curtain that looks as if it has a separate valance, select fabric with no apparent right or wrong side. For sheer and lightweight fabrics, use triple fullness across the window. To save time, do not piece panels together; using the full fabric width, sew each panel separately. Install all the panels on a single curtain rod or pole, arranging the sides of the panels so they fall inside the draped fabric folds.

To determine the length of each curtain panel, add a total of 24" (61 cm) to the finished length, measured from the top of the rod. This amount includes allowances for a 2" (5 cm) heading, and a rod pocket casing 2" (5 cm) deep to fit a 1½" (3.8 cm) diameter curtain rod. The finished length of the valance from heading to hem is 14" (35.5 cm).

To prepare each panel for the flip top heading, make double side hems. If the selvages have a finished look, side hems can be omitted on the inner panels.

How to Make a Flip Top Heading

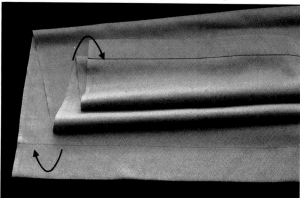

1) Stitch a double hem toward *right* side at top of curtain panel. Stitch a double hem toward *wrong* side at lower edge of curtain.

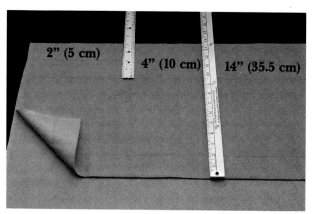

2) Fold top of panel over to right side to create valance 14" (35.5 cm) long. Mark stitching line 2" (5 cm) from fold for heading and 4" (10 cm) from fold for rod pocket. Stitch on marked lines.

Tie Top Curtains

Refreshingly casual, a tied heading is appropriate for sill-length or full-length curtains. Make ties from matching or coordinating fabric, or save time by using 1½" to 2" (3.8 to 5 cm) wide ribbon.

For the curtain, use 1½ to 2 times the finished width for fabric fullness. To determine the finished length, measure from bottom of the rod to the desired length. Allow enough extra fabric for double side and lower hems, plus ½" (1.3 cm) seam allowance at

the top of each panel. Also cut a 4" (10 cm) facing as long as the finished width of the panel. To prepare each panel for the tie top heading, make double side hems and a double lower hem.

For each tie, you will need a 4" by 10" (10 by 25.5 cm) strip. Cut longer ties if you want to make bows instead of knots. Determine the number of ties needed by placing one pair at each end of a curtain panel, one pair in the center, and spacing the remaining pairs of ties at 6" to 8" (15 to 20.5 cm) intervals. Cut ties efficiently with a rotary cutter; cut 4" (10 cm) wide strips as long as possible; then cut the strips into separate ties.

How to Sew a Tie Top Heading

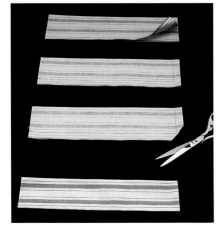

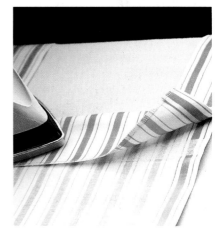

1) Fold strip lengthwise, right sides together, and stitch across one short end and along long edge with ½" (1.3 cm) seam allowance; or overlock. Use continuous stitching. Trim corner, turn right side out, and press.

2) Pin pairs of ties to right side of curtain with raw edges even. Overlock one long edge of facing, or hem with narrow hem. Pin facing strip over ties, with right sides of facing and curtain together. Stitch ½" (1.3 cm) seam at top of facing.

3) Turn facing to wrong side, so ties are free at upper edge. Fold raw edges of facing under ½" (1.3 cm) on each side. Fuse side and lower edges to curtain with fusible web.

Valances

Balloon valance. A balloon valance, above, gives simple sheers or draperies a soft, casual look. This valance, with bottom hem draped into swags, looks complicated but is actually easy to sew. It is a basic rod pocket curtain, shortened to valance length. Each swag is created with shade tape or by tying cord through plastic rings. The balloon valance can be used on a curtain rod, a cafe pole, or a Continental™ rod.

For graceful draping, make balloon valances about 28" (71 cm) long. To determine cut length, add to the finished length allowances for the heading, rod pocket, and double lower hem. To determine cut width, allow triple fullness if using sheer or lightweight fabric, or 2 to 2½ times fullness for medium-weight decorator fabrics; allow for double side hems.

Flat valance. A flat valance, right, takes little fabric and even less sewing time. It is a plain fabric panel with rod pockets for a pair of curtain rods. The simple, tailored style of this valance can complement contemporary or traditional decor. Choose a medium to heavyweight fabric with a crisp, firm hand; or back lightweight fabric with a layer of fusible interfacing. Textured fabrics such as cotton jacquard, raw silk, cotton velvet, and synthetic suede are appropriate as are quilted fabrics and needlework such as trapunto.

To determine cut length, install the rods so the distance between them equals the desired finished length. Most valances are made 12" to 14" (30.5 to 35.5 cm) long, depending on the proportion to window size. To measure, pin a tape measure around the top rod, down, and around the bottom rod. Add 1"

(2.5 cm) for turning under the raw edges. To determine the cut width of a flat valance, measure the length of the curtain rod, including returns. Add 3" (7.5 cm) for side hems.

Puff valance. A puff valance, right, has a light, airy look. It is a natural for sheers and other lightweight fabrics. Combine a puff valance with shades, curtains, or blinds for a layered window treatment, or use it alone as a decorative accent.

This valance is made from a strip of fabric cut large enough to form a self-lining. To determine cut length, double the finished length of the valance; add heading and rod pocket allowances. To determine cut width, use triple fabric fullness for sheer and lightweight fabric or 2½ times the finished width for mediumweight fabric; add 4" (10 cm) for double side hems.

How to Sew a Balloon Valance

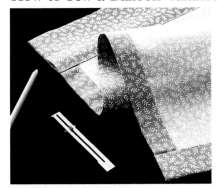 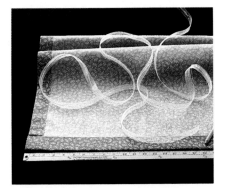 

1) Make double side and bottom hems. Turn upper raw edge under ½" (1.3 cm), and press. Fold edge over to form heading and rod pocket; mark stitching lines. Stitch as marked.

2) Mark location for shade tape at lower edge of shade. Swags should hang at even intervals across valance, about 8" to 12" (20.5 to 30.5 cm) apart; if width is double fabric fullness, tapes should be 16" to 24" (40.5 to 61 cm) apart.

3) Cut strips of shade tape 24" (61 cm) long, making sure that the first tack over the cord is at the top of the hem. Stitch tape in place. Pull up cord from both ends, and tie. Tuck cords into swag.

How to Sew a Flat Valance

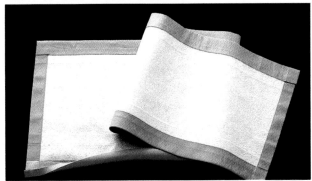 

1) Turn under raw edges at sides ½" (1.3 cm). Press. Turn under 1" (2.5 cm), and stitch side hems. Fold fabric to wrong side to form rod pockets on upper and lower edges, turning under raw edges ½" (1.3 cm). Stitch rod pockets.

2) Insert rods through rod pocket at top and bottom to install valance at window. Valance takes shape of rods and has custom upholstered look. For quick trim, fuse grosgrain ribbon over stitching lines.

How to Sew a Puff Valance

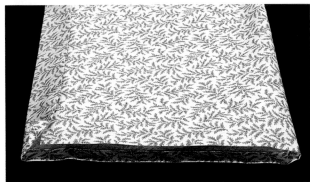 

1) Make double side hems. Turn upper raw edge under ½" (1.3 cm), and press. Fold edge over to depth of heading. Bring lower raw edge up, and lap ½" (1.3 cm) under heading. Stitch along folded edge to form heading. Stitch parallel row below folded edge to form rod pocket.

2) Slip rod through rod pocket to install valance. Pull fabric layers apart along length of valance to create puffs. If valance seems limp, stuff with tissue paper or plastic drycleaning bags for fuller look.

Swags with Side Drapes

This swag is a valance draped across the top of a window, with a fabric drape at the sides. Swags can be draped from post-type drapery holdbacks mounted at or above the corners of a window frame, or they can be draped around decorative finials at the ends of curtain rods.

To simplify the construction of the elegant and graceful lined swag (right), shape a fabric panel to size with two easy window measurements. Measure the width between holdbacks or finials. Measure finished length from top of hardware to point on side of window where you want the drape to end. The cut length of panel equals the width, plus twice the length, plus 1" (2.5 cm) for seam allowances. Line the panel to the edge to eliminate hems and headings; then use shirring tape to gather the fabric for draping. To save cutting time, cut the decorator fabric and lining together.

Save even more time by making a swagged valance or curtain from a fabric with no apparent right or wrong side, such as gauze, handkerchief linen, silk broadcloth, or lace. Drape artfully over a decorative rod. There is no need to line or shirr the panel. To finish edges and ends, fuse or glue hems for a custom look without taking a stitch. Swag can also be tied to finials with separate bows or tasseled cords.

How to Make a No-sew Swag

1) Drape tape measure across window between finials of decorative rod to estimate finished width of swag. Measure finished length. The cut length of panel equals the finished width, plus twice the finished length, plus two hem allowances; allow extra fabric for draping adjustments.

2) Drape fabric over rod to test effect. If fabric panel is too wide, trim side edges for desired effect. Mark hems, and fuse or glue them. Drape finished panel over rod, and adjust fabric into soft folds. Tie cord around folds at corners to hold in place. Knot soft or slippery fabrics around finials to anchor swag.

How to Sew Lined Swag with Side Drape

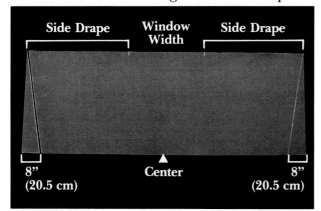

1) Measure and mark center and window width. On opposite side, mark 8" (20.5 cm) in from each corner. Layer decorator fabric and lining, and cut diagonally to opposite corner on each side.

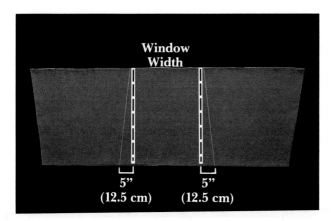

2) Sew lining to panel, with right sides together. At center of shorter edge, leave an opening for turning. Trim corners. Turn right side out; press. Fuse or glue opening closed. On lining, mark shorter edge of panel 5" (12.5 cm) out from the width markings.

3) Position 2-cord shirring tape on diagonal lines from window width mark on long side to 5" (12.5 cm) mark on short side.

4) Stitch shirring tape between each set of marks. Knot cords of tape at shorter edge. Pull up cords to gather swag. Mount on drapery holdbacks and adjust folds.

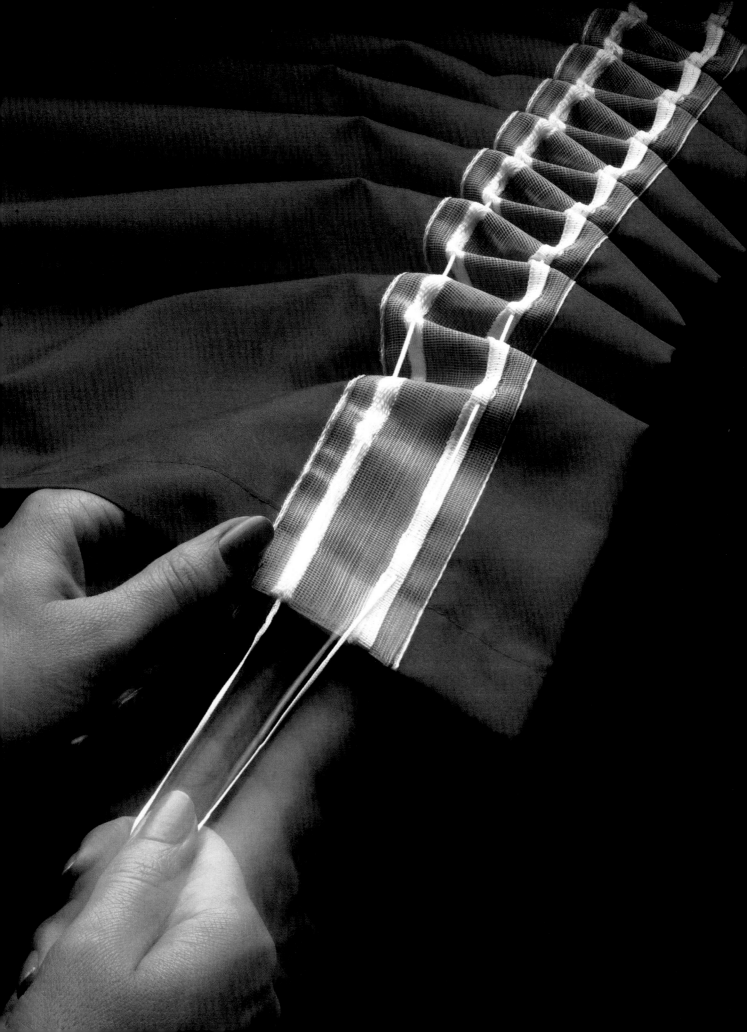

Shortcut Curtain & Valance Headings

The timesaving way to sew decorative curtain, drapery, and valance headings is with self-styling tape. The tapes are simply stitched flat to hemmed panels and woven-in cords are pulled to create the heading. For best results, use these tapes on medium to lightweight or sheer fabrics.

To estimate the amount of fabric needed, measure the width of the rod, including rod returns, if any. Multiply by 2½ for fabric fullness for the pleating or the folding tape. Multiply by 2½ or 3 for fullness for the smocking or shirring tapes. Lightweight and sheer fabrics are more luxurious with more fullness. Add an allowance for double side hems to determine how wide to cut the fabric panels. Divide total by width of fabric for the number of widths needed.

Measure finished length of curtain and add 6" (15 cm) for double 3" (7.5 cm) bottom hem and 1" to 5" (2.5 to 12.5 cm) for the top hem, depending on style of tape or rod being used. Add another 2" (5 cm) for a double top hem on sheer fabrics.

Multiply length by the number of widths needed and divide by 36" (100 cm) for the number of yards (meters) required. Add 6" (15 cm) to finished width to determine how much tape to buy for each panel.

To hang the finished panels, use standard metal drapery pins or special hooks that fit into loops woven into the top of the shirring tape. As an option, on smocked or shirred headings you can make a rod pocket to hang curtain or valance on flat curtain rod or pole and omit hooks or pins.

Curtain and drapery headings are quick and easy to make with self-styling tapes. Pinch pleats, box pleats, shirring, and smocking are possible with the least amount of measuring and sewing.

Matching tiebacks for shirred or smocked window treatments are easy to make, using the same type of tape selected for the heading. Simply apply the tape to the wrong side of a fabric strip, and pull the cords to shirr or smock to size.

Self-styling Tapes for Curtain, Drapery, and Valance Headings

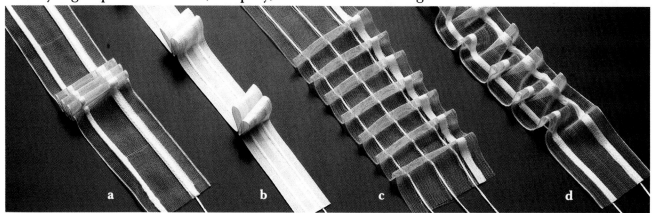

Self-styling cords and hook loops are woven into tapes for a variety of curtain, drapery, and valance headings. Use pleating tape **(a)** for soft pleated headings for draw draperies on sheers, laces, and lightweight fabrics. Folding tape **(b)** makes a two-pleat heading, appropriate to small windows, or a 3" (7.5 cm) box pleat for dust ruffles and valances. Shirring tape **(c)** draws curtain panels into narrow, evenly spaced pencil pleats. Smocking tape **(d)** creates soft alternating pleats for a smocked look.

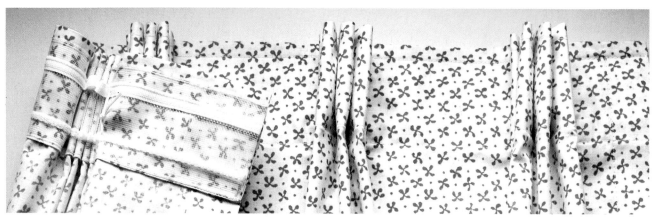

Pleating tape is used for classic pinch pleats to hang on a traverse rod or a decorative pole rod with cafe rings. For decorative and cafe rods, press under 1½" (3.8 cm) on top edge. Stitch tape ½" (1.3 cm) from edge. For traverse rods, turn under 1" (2.5 cm) and stitch tape ¼" (6 mm) from edge. For draw draperies, arrange the pleating tape so pleats do not form at the ends of the panel. Also allow 4" to 5" (10 to 12.5 cm) at end of drapery panels for overlap at center of rod.

Folding tape is used for a tailored two-pleat heading or box pleats. Because the two-pleat heading stacks compactly, this heading is well-suited for recreational vehicles and boats as well as residential window treatments. Stitch and hang finished panels as for pinch pleats with pleating tape, above.

Box pleats are also made with folding tape. Stitch tape on *right* side of fabric ½" (1.3 cm) from upper edge. Pull cords to create pleats. From right side, flatten and press the pleats. For pleated valance, stitch mounting flap of lining or matching fabric below tape. Turn under and staple valance to a mounting board, or insert curtain hooks and hang on a flat curtain rod. For dust ruffle, stitch muslin deck to pleated panel.

Smocking tape creates a stationary window treatment with soft smocked folds. Hang finished panels on cafe rod, decorative pole rod with cafe rings, or flat curtain rod. To hang on a flat curtain rod, insert metal drapery hook every 3" (7.5 cm). Or, make panels with rod pocket, using method given for shirred heading on page 115. Two rows of smocking tape can be applied for extra-deep heading if desired.

Shirring tape is used to draw up fabric panels evenly into soft folds. Select this heading for stationary window treatments such as tieback draperies, curtains, and valances. Hang the finished panels on a decorative pole rod with glides, a cafe rod with rings, or a flat curtain rod. Smocked and shirred headings may be 2½ to 3 times fullness.

How to Sew a Heading with Self-styling Tapes

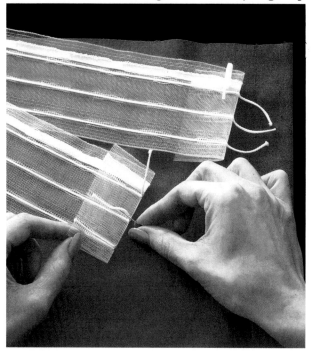

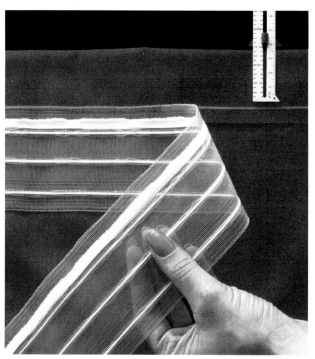

1) Cut tape to match width of hemmed panel. Turn under 1½" (3.8 cm) on ends of tape, and use pin to pick out cords. Side of tape with hook loops is right side of tape.

2) Turn under 2" (5 cm) along top of panel. Press. Position tape, right side up, on wrong side of panel 1½" (3.8 cm) from fold. Make sure edge of tape with hook loops is toward top of panel. Stitch top and bottom edges of tape. Do not catch cords.

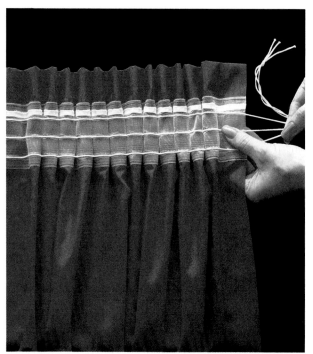

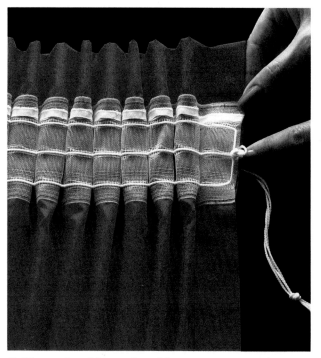

3) Secure cords at both ends of tape, using one or two overhand knots to prevent cords from being pulled out. Pull cords at one end to gather fabric as tightly as possible; then adjust gathers to distribute them evenly, and ease out heading to width desired.

4) Tie cords with overhand knot to secure gathers. Tie excess cord in half bow knot, and conceal behind panel. To launder or clean panel, untie cords and smooth out heading to make panel flat and easier to handle.

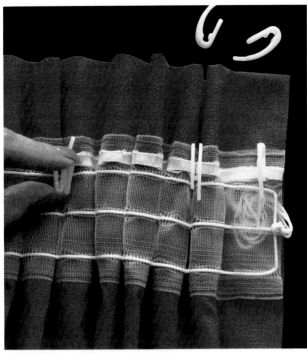

5) Insert special two-pronged drapery/curtain hooks into hook loops, spacing hooks about 3" (7.5 cm) apart. Special hooks are made by manufacturer of shirring tape.

6) Insert hooks into eyes of cafe rings or glides of decorative rod. For flat curtain rod, insert standard metal drapery pins into hook loops on tape.

How to Sew Self-styling Tape Heading with Rod Pocket

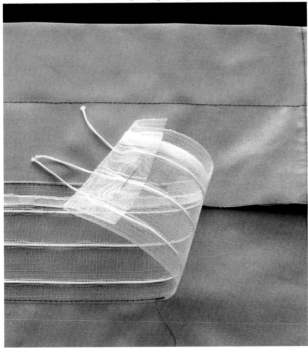

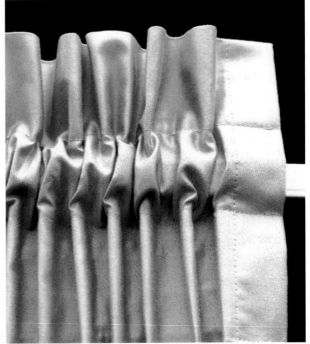

1) Make rod pocket and heading, allowing raw edge to extend ½" (1.3 cm) below lower stitching line for rod pocket. Prepare shirring tape as in step 1. Position upper edge of shirring tape at lower stitching line for rod pocket, and stitch in place.

2) Form shirred heading as in steps 3 and 4. Insert rod in rod pocket.

Decorating with Lace

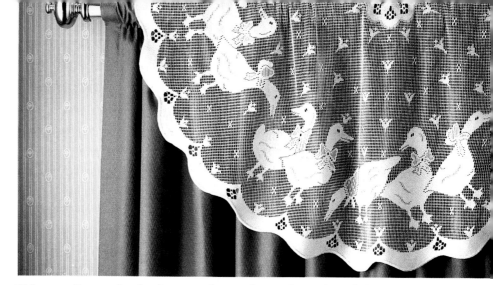

Valances. Drape circular lace panel over decorative pole rod for a timesaving valance. Use purchased round tablecloth, or cut circle from allover lace. No hems are necessary.

Tieback curtains. Stitch rod pocket heading on lace panel. Insert rod, and hang panel. Tie bow or tieback around lace. To make a bishop's sleeve curtain, use lace panel that is about 24" (61 cm) longer than measurement from rod to floor. Attach one or two tiebacks, and puff up lace panel to create bishop's sleeve effect. Allow lower edge to puddle gracefully onto floor.

Pillows. Slipcover pillows with tie-on lace cases to refresh a solid-color pillow. Cut lace sections to size of pillow plus ½" (1.3 cm) for seams. Stitch lace square on three sides. Use ribbon to tie fourth side closed.

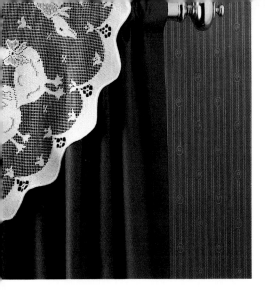

Tied panels. Thread satin or grosgrain ribbon through tops of lace panels. To hang panels, tie bows or knots over decorative curtain or shower rod.

Lampshades and shutters. Gather lace over lampshade frame. Staple lace panels behind shutter openings or to the frame of a folding screen.

Table toppers. Cut a lace circle, or purchase a round lace tablecloth. Trim edge with ruffled wide-lace trim, or divide edge into 6 to 8 sections and gather into swags. To show off lace pattern most effectively, layer lace over solid-color or printed floor-length cloth.

Quick Pillows

Four Timesaving Pillows

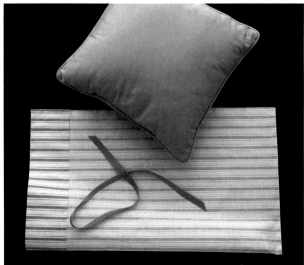

Sack pillow. Cut a 30" (76 cm) square. Turn under a deep hem on one side and fuse or stitch in place. Fold in half with right sides together and stitch raw edges together. Turn right side out. Insert pillow and tie a ribbon around open end.

Tie-on cover. Overlock the edge of large lace or decorator fabric square, or hem with narrow hem. Or make reversible slipcover by using two fabrics back to back. Tack ribbon tie or decorative cord at each corner. Lay pillow diagonally on slipcover, and fold corners over pillow. Tie closed.

Wrapped neckroll. Cut large fabric rectangle. Overlock raw edges, or hem with narrow hem. Wrap around foam bolster form or rolled quilt batt. Roll up excess fabric at each end, and tack. Tie ribbon or cord around rolled fabric.

Slip-on cover. Overlock one edge of both pillow cover sections, or hem with narrow hem. With right sides together, stitch remaining three sides in ½" (1.3 cm) seam. Clip corners. Turn right side out. Tack ribbon ties to open side. Insert fabric-covered pillow, and tie ribbons into bows.

Placemats & Napkins

With timesaving fabrics and speedy sewing techniques, you can create a variety of placemats and napkins for special occasions and gifts. For casual dining, choose loosely woven fabric, such as linen or homespun, and fringe the edges. For a more formal look, choose fabric with a finer weave, and finish edges with a dense flatlock, zigzag, or decorative machine embroidery stitch and contrasting thread. Woven plaids and geometric designs are especially timesaving, because you can follow a design or woven line to eliminate marking.

Bias-bound edges are always appropriate on napkins and placemats, as are rolled or satin edges sewn on an overlock machine. When sewing bound, rolled, or satin edges, you can easily make placemats and napkins reversible by using two contrasting fabrics. The double layers not only give you two looks for the sewing time, but also provide extra absorbency. If desired, add a layer of lightweight polyester fleece for padding between the two fabric faces of a reversible placemat.

To save time when binding edges, cut a continuous bias strip long enough to finish several items; a 36" (91.5 cm) fabric square will yield a continuous bias strip about 17 yards (16.2 m) long and 2" (5 cm) wide. Fold under and press the raw edges of the strip quickly with a bias tape pressing aid.

How to Make a Continuous Bias Strip

1) Mark each crosswise grain edge of a large fabric square with *one* pin. Mark each lengthwise grain edge with *two* pins.

2) Fold fabric in half diagonally on the true bias grain of fabric. Cut on fold line to divide square into two triangles.

3) Stitch lengthwise grain edges (double pins) in ¼" (6 mm) seam with right sides together. Allow points to extend ¼" (6 mm), so edges meet exactly on seamline. Press seam open.

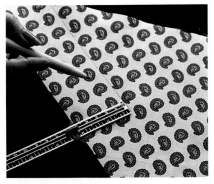

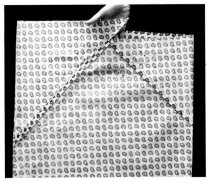

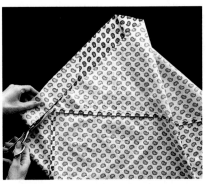

4) Mark cutting line for bias strip parallel to one slanted edge on right side of fabric. This edge is on true bias grain of fabric.

5) Pin crosswise grain edges (single pins) together with one edge extending beyond the other edge the marked width of the bias strip. This creates a slightly twisted tube. Stitch and press ¼" (6 mm) seam.

6) Cut fabric on marked line. As you cut, fold cut portion of strip over to use as a cutting guide. Continue folding strip back and cutting around tube to the end.

How to Use Bias Tape Maker

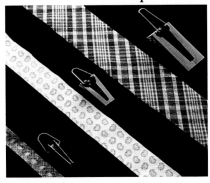

1) Cut bias strip according to size of tape maker. Cut strip scant 1" (2.5 cm) wide for ½" (1.3 cm) tape maker, 1⅜" (3.5 cm) wide for ¾" (2 cm) tape maker, 1⅞" (4.7 cm) wide for 1" (2.5 cm) tape maker, or scant 3¼" (8.2 cm) wide for 2" (5 cm) tape maker.

2) Trim one end of bias strip to a point. Thread point through channel at wide end of tape maker, bringing point out at narrow end. Insert pin in slot opening to pull point through. Pin point of strip to pressing surface.

3) Press folded bias strip as you pull tape maker the length of strip. Tape maker automatically folds raw edges to center of strip to create uniform bias tape quickly.

How to Apply Bias Binding to an Oval Placemat

1) Press bias tape in half to form double-fold bias binding. Press binding into curved shape to match shape of mat. To prevent puckering and remove slack, stretch binding slightly as you press.

2) Baste placemat to backing, *wrong* sides together, with glue stick. Dab small dots of glue stick around edge of placemat on right side. Finger press one edge of binding into position. Baste other edge of binding to backing with glue stick.

3) Join binding ends by opening fold and trimming across end. Fold cut edge under ¼" (6 mm). Lap over other end of binding, and baste lightly with glue stick.

4) Stitch along inner edge of binding with straight or zigzag stitches. The Even Feed™ foot may also be used to keep layers from shifting.

Shortcut Napkins or Placemats on an Overlock Machine

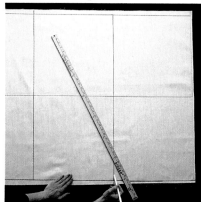

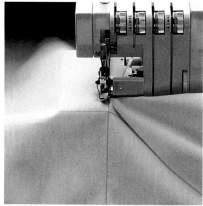

1) Mark cutting lines for finished size of napkins or placemats. You can make six 15" (38 cm) square napkins from 1 yard (.95 m) of 45" (115 cm) wide fabric.

2) Adjust overlock machine for narrow 3-thread stitch or rolled edge. Stitch on all lengthwise cutting lines. Then stitch on all crosswise cutting lines.

3) Apply liquid fray preventer to threads at each corner. After fray preventer dries, trim threads.

How to Make Fringed Placemats or Napkins

1) Cut placemat to the desired finished size. Mark a stitching line ½" (1.3 cm) from raw edges to indicate depth of fringe, or use a line from a check or plaid.

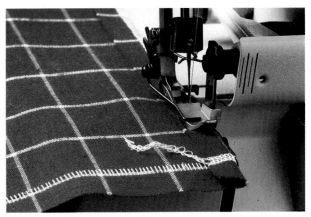

2) Fold one side on the marked line. Set overlock machine for flatlock stitch; sew along fold. Do not allow knives to cut into fold. Open fold to pull stitches flat. Flatlock remaining sides the same way.

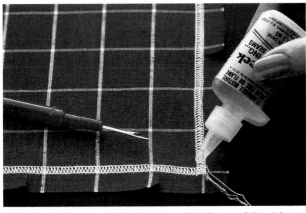

3) Seal stitches at each corner with drop of liquid fray preventer. Use seam ripper to remove stitches in fringe area. Cut up to stitches every 3" (7.5 cm). Remove threads to create fringe.

Alternative method. On conventional machine, use satin stitching or closely spaced zigzag stitches. Stitch on marked lines; pivot at corners. Cut up to stitches every 3" (7.5 cm). Remove threads to create fringe.

How to Make Reversible Napkins or Placemats

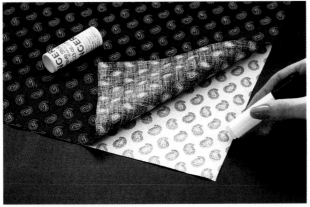

1) Cut napkin or placemat and contrasting backing the same size. Layer them, *wrong* sides together, so edges match. Use glue stick to hold layers together.

2) Adjust overlock machine for 3-thread stitch or rolled hem. On conventional machine, use satin stitching or overedge stitching. Stitch around all sides, handling the two layers as one.

Tie chair seat cushions in place with bows.

Use bows on curtain tiebacks.

Use bows to accent table toppers or swags.

Bows & Knots

One of the easiest ways to accent a decorating scheme or give a new look is with large, soft bows or knots. At the window, use bows or knots to trim the corners of swags, to shape drapery or curtain panels into pouffed tiers, and to tie valances into draped scallops for a swag or cloud effect. Streamers, 16" to 20" (40.5 to 51 cm) long, give a luxurious effect.

In addition, bows or knots are a quick alternative to more tailored curtain and drapery tiebacks. To use as tiebacks on ruffled curtains, slit the panel next to the ruffle and seal the cut edges with liquid fray preventer; tie a bow through the slit, so the ruffle is not crushed. Sew a small plastic ring to the center of the bow, or knot the section to use as a tieback. You can also use bows or knots to trim lampshades and to anchor seat cushions on chairs.

The speediest bows or knots can be sewn from one continuous tube of fabric. Cut the tube into appropriate sections as needed. For best results, use lightweight fabric with a crisp finish. To add body to limp fabrics, apply soft fusible interfacing to the wrong side of the fabric before cutting and sewing.

How to Sew a One-piece Bow or Knot

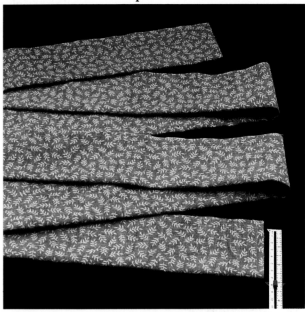

1) Cut strips 7" (18 cm) wide for 3" (7.5 cm) wide bows or knots, and 9" (23 cm) wide for 4" (10 cm) wide bows or knots. Cut strips as long as possible, so multiple bows or knots can be cut from each strip. Fold strip in half lengthwise, right sides together. Sew seam on one long edge. Turn right side out, and press.

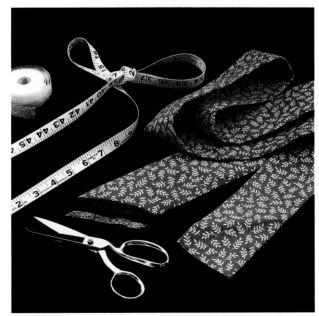

2) Cut strip into bow-length or knot-length sections. Determine length of sections by tying tape measure into bow or knot for desired effect. Cut ends of sections at an angle. Fold raw edges into tube, and press. Fuse or glue openings closed.

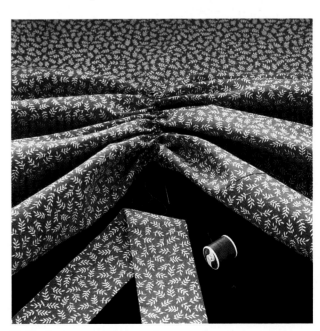

3) Tack center of bow or knot section to seat cushion and tie. Or, for tiebacks or swags, tie bow before attaching.

Index

For additional information about the
Waverly decorator fabrics shown on pages
100-125, please write to:
  Waverly
  79 Madison Avenue
  New York, NY 10016
  Attention: Public Relations Dept.